World Word B

A Guide to

Foreign Words

CU00659621

The **One Hour Wordpower** *series*

One Hour Wordpower

World Word Bank
A Guide to Foreign Words and Sayings

GRAHAM KING

Mandarin
in association with
The Sunday Times

A Mandarin Paperback
WORLD WORD BANK

First published in Great Britain 1994
by Mandarin Paperbacks
an imprint of Reed Consumer Books Ltd
Michelin House, 81 Fulham Road, London SW3 6RB
and Auckland, Melbourne, Singapore and Toronto

Copyright © Graham King 1994
The right of Graham King to be identified
as the Author of these works has been asserted
in accordance with the Copyright, Designs
and Patents Act 1988

A CIP catalogue record for this title
is available from the British Library
ISBN 0 7493 1880 5

Printed and bound in Great Britain
by Cox & Wyman, Reading, Berks.

Contents

Acknowledgements

The author owes a debt to the many sources sifted through for this compilation. Although the primary sources were various foreign dictionaries, the following works were especially useful and are commended:

Dictionary of Foreign Phrases and Classical Quotations ed. H. P. Jones (John Grant); *Dictionary of Foreign Terms and Phrases* by C. O. S. Mawson, ed. Eugene Ehrlich (Penguin); *A Dictionary of Foreign Words and Phrases in Current English* by Alan Bliss (Routledge); *Foreign Expressions* by B. A. Phythian (Headway: Hodder & Stoughton); *Concise Dictionary of 26 Languages* by Peter M. Bergman (Signet); *French False Friends* by C. W. E. Kirk-Greene (Routledge & Kegan Paul).

On idiomatic usage, Cassell's series on colloquial French, German, Italian and Spanish proved to be excellent reference books and are easily the best in this field. Harrap's *Anglais-Français Slang Dictionnaire* and Genevieve's idiosyncratic *Merde!* (HarperCollins/ Fontana) were trawled for some rude bits, while a few samplings from Henry Beard's *Latin for All Occasions* (Angus & Robertson) bring a dead language to life in a most engaging way.

Also consulted were Hugo's *Simplified System Phrase Books* (Hugo's Language Books Limited); Collins' *Traveller* phrase books and dictionaries (William Collins & Co); Barron's Educational Series and *Instant Foreign Language Programs for Travelers*; and Berlitz's phrase books and dictionaries (Berlitz Publishing Co Ltd).

Consultant on Linguistics: Paul Coggle, Senior Lecturer in German, University of Kent at Canterbury.

Evening Standard

Monday, 13 December, 1993

Quis custodiet . . .

MRS VIRGINIA BOTTOMLEY might have seemed immune to the tidal wave of criticism about the way her NHS reforms have reduced the number of people who make patients better and increased the number of managers who administer the way they do it. But, in fact, she is responding to the charges. Her answer to the people who complained about the new breed of bureaucrats with excessive pay and perks is to invent yet another sort of bureaucrat. She has ordered a "task force" to investigate the remuneration deals of NHS managers.

Certainly, something had to be done. The revelation that the number of nurses in London has gone down by 5,000 over the last three years, while the number of managers has trebled, is an indictment of the way the reforms have misfired. But inventing a task force to investigate the administrators isn't quite the solution the critics had in mind. What will happen if it turns out that the people running the task-force are over-paid and over-numerous? Will there be a task force to investigate the task force? And will the administrators sacked as NHS managers find new, lucrative jobs as investigators?

Do you know your Latin, French and Japanese?

Here are excerpts from editorials in two British newspapers.

In one, the editorial is headlined with an incomplete Latin quotation: *quis custodiet ipsos custodes?* In context it is entirely appropriate – but how many readers would have known what it means?

In the second, not one but two foreign expressions are used in a single paragraph – one French and one Japanese. Most readers are familiar with one, but the other. . . ?

These, and a couple of thousand other foreign words, expressions and quotations will be found in this book.

19 DECEMBER 1993

THE OBSERVER

e as-
ig the
quon-
orman

ky mo-
ll tele-
when
brity.
le a

'I enjoyed the evening enormously,' a remark that is hard to decode as an attack on the mischievous Clary.

But the *faux pas* has now triggered a *tsunami* of homophobia.

The self-selecting taste arbiters of the tabloid press — all of whom were

be. 10, acco
dissident Tory
'The real probl
tionist queers s
Clary. They giv
a bad name.' I
the *Daily Star*
blue comic P
was shock
praved j

9

Introduction

The great grammarian H. W. Fowler didn't mince his
words on the practice of using foreign terms and
expressions designed to go over the heads of the
average English reader. 'To use French words,' he
wrote, 'that your reader or hearer does not know or
does not fully understand . . . is inconsiderate and rude.
Display of superior knowledge is as great a vulgarity
as display of superior wealth.'

Nevertheless, this infusion of foreign expressions
into our reading, in newspapers, magazines and books,
is a fact of life whether we like it or not. We have the
choice, when encountering yet another burst of
italics, of groaning and fetching the dictionary, with
an excellent chance of searching in vain for the word
or phrase, or blithely leaping over the intrusion and
reading on, saddled with guilt and ignorance.

Perhaps we should remind ourselves that English,
in any case, is a language that over the centuries has
picked up words like a magnet picks up iron filings,
so nothing has really changed. Take *Schadenfreude*, a
German word meaning 'taking malicious pleasure
from another's misfortune'. A decade or so ago you'd
never have seen this word in print; now it's everywhere.
In fact it is now considered to be naturalized into the
language, it has lost its German capital 'S', it is
featured in most English dictionaries and fewer
writers bother to italicize it any more.

That process has been repeated with thousands of
words, terms and sayings from other languages. Many
of them are now so embedded in English that we
simply couldn't do without them. Like *tête-à-tête*, *vis-
à-vis*, *bête noir* and *bon mot* from the French; *ad hoc*,
'et cetera' and *post mortem* from Latin; 'leitmotiv',
gesundheit and 'wunderkind' from German;
'ombudsman' from Swedish', not to mention several

hundred musical and operatic terms from Italian.

Perhaps this cherry-picking is a reflection of our ineptitude with other languages, for we are, among Europeans, at the bottom of the linguistic league, only a whisker ahead of Ireland. The proportion of Britons able to speak a foreign language is the lowest in the EU, where almost 100% of young people in Luxembourg, Denmark and Holland can speak a second language, most often English.

World Word Bank is not going to rectify the situation, but it may help us when we encounter a foreign word or saying which we do not understand. Indeed, it may even encourage some of us to actually use, with confidence, the odd *mot juste* in letters or reports or in our everyday speech.

No compilation of this kind, least of all *World Word Bank*, can ever claim to include every foreign word, phrase or quotation waiting to trip us up. With over 2,500 languages in the world, and with many of them containing hundreds, if not thousands, of words that might express a thought more aptly or colourfully or economically than our home-grown variety, such a collection is impossible to imagine.

But here, at least, is a concise selection that should prove useful to the contemporary reader and writer. It excludes many foreign words that now reside in any good comprehensive dictionary. It also excludes specialist terms, including those connected with music, opera and ballet; these will be found in most English dictionaries. On the other hand it includes a good many colloquial and even vulgar expressions not to be found in dictionaries but which are common enough in speech and print. The rationale behind *World Word Bank* is relevance to contemporary needs.

In the spirit of the *One Hour Wordpower* series of books on English usage and effective communication, the tone here is light, even light-hearted, and leavened throughout with intriguing and humorous observations on the world's languages and how we use them.

A Note on Pronunciation

The English or Continental pronunciation of Roman spelling has been used to convey, as far as possible, the sounds of words belonging to languages with non-Latin alphabets: Russian, Greek, Hebrew, Arabic, Japanese and Chinese (Pinyin).

Words and phrases which are often used orally amidst the English language (*après-ski*, *fruits de mer*, *nisi*, *repêchage* etc.) are accompanied by an indication of their pronunciation. As this guide is intended for English speakers, pronunciation is indicated by simple letter combinations like STY, HAY, GO, BOO and AK:

adieu	ah-DYUR
ex gratia	eks GRAH-shuh
mêlée	meh-lay
sine die	see-nay dee-ay

There are some traps. Words ending in '**-y**' may be pronounced differently:

early	ER-lee	(the 'long e' sound)
layby	LAY-by	(the 'long i' sound)

To make the difference clear, the 'long e' sound is indicated by 'ee' to rhyme with **glee**, and the 'long i' sound by a 'y' to rhyme with **eye**.

A stressed syllable is capitalized:

kaffeeklatsch	KAF-ay-klatsh

Perhaps the biggest problem facing English speakers is French nasalization. Nasalization – horrible word!

– results in losing the end of a word in a combination of a sneer and a snort.

One nasalized sound is that which combines an 's' and a 'z' resulting in the softly sibilant 's' in **leisure** and **vision**. This sound is indicated by the combination 'zh':

mélange	may-LARNZH
protégé	PROT-eh-zhay

The more difficult sound is that required to pronounce correctly words like *vin* and *blanc de blancs*. Most people manage to produce a sound like 'vahng' for the former, which isn't too far off the mark, and 'blonk duh blonk' for the latter, which all but pedants find acceptable. But if you wish to do better you could try to nasalize the ends of the syllables, and to indicate this we have used the following device:

blanc de blancs	blah(n) duh blah(n)
en passant	an(n) PAS-sah(n)
coquilles St Jacques	koh-khee sah(n) zhahk

The (n) indicates that the preceding vowel sounds should be followed by an 'ng' sound that somehow gets lost up the nose. If you listen to a fluent French speaker, or to a language tape, you should get the idea fairly quickly.

Guide to Abbreviations

Abor	Australian Aborigine
Ch	Chinese
Dut	Dutch
Fr	French
Gael	Gaelic
Ger	German
Gk	Greek
Heb	Hebrew
Hun	Hungarian
Ir	Irish
It	Italian
Jap	Japanese
Lat	Latin
Pers	Persian
Port	Portuguese
Rus	Russian
Scand	Scandinavian
Scot	Scottish
Sp	Spanish
Swed	Swedish
Turk	Turkish
Yid	Yiddish

World Word Bank

A

à bientôt [Fr] (ah-byah(n)-toh)
Goodbye – see you again soon.

abseil [Ger] (AB-seyl)
Descending a steep or vertical surface using a double rope which is recovered by the last climber down.

accidia [Lat from Gk]
Spiritual apathy and indifference. Has been anglicized to **accidie**.

accouchement [Fr] (ah-koosh-mah(n)
Period of confinement for childbirth.

à chacun son goût [Fr]
Every man to his taste.

acushla [Ir] (ah-KOOSH-luh)
Darling: term of endearment. The term **macushla** (my pulse; my heartbeart) is an anglicism.

Adeste, fideles [Lat] (ad-EST-tay fih-DAY-lees)
First line of the hymn known as 'O come, all ye faithful'.

à deux [Fr] (ah-DUR)
For two; a meal for two; a meeting between two people, etc.

ad hoc [Lat]
For a particular purpose only; something hastily arranged.

adieu [Fr] (ah-DYU)
>Farewell.

ad infinitum [Lat]
>To infinity; without end.

ad interim [Lat]
>For the meantime.

adiós [Sp] (ad-YOHS)
>Farewell.

ad libitum; **ad lib** [Lat]
>At a performer's discretion; to improvise and speak or perform without preparation.

ad nauseam [Lat]
>To a sickening degree.

affaire [Fr]
>Affair; scandal.

affaire d'amour [Fr]
>Love affair.

affaire de cœur [Fr]
>Love affair; affair of the heart.

affaire d'honneur [Fr] (uh-FAYR doh-NUR)
>A matter of honour.

affiche [Fr]
>A poster or notice.

aficionado [Sp] (ah-feess-yuh-NAR-doh)
>An ardent enthusiast; in Spain, of bull-fighting.

à fond [Fr]
>Thoroughly; to the end; to the bottom.

a fortiori [Lat] (ay-for-tih-OR-ih)
>All the more; for similar but sounder reasons.

agent provocateur [Fr]
>   (Ah-zhar(n) prov-ok-uh-TUR)
>Someone who provokes another to commit a crime to provide evidence for a conviction.

à gogo [Fr]
>In abundance; galore.

agrégation [Fr] (ag-rah-GAS-yor(n))
>The ***concours d'agregation*** is the French competitive examination for teaching posts.

aide-de-camp [Fr] (ay-duh-kah(n))
> Personal assistant to a senior military officer.

aide-mémoire [Fr] (ayd-mem-wuh)
> Notes to help the memory.

aîné [Fr] *ay-nay*
> Elder; always preceded by a name.

aïoli [Fr]
> A widely used garlic sauce.

akvavit
> See ***aquavit***.

à la carte [Fr]
> A menu where each dish is priced separately.

à la mode [Fr]
> Fashionable.

à la recherche du temps perdu [Fr]
> Marcel Proust's seven-part novel is usually
> known in English as *Remembrance of Things Past*.

al dente [It] (al-DEN-tey)
> Cooked to retain firmness (usually pasta); not
> too soft.

al fresco; ***alfresco*** [It]
> In the open air.

allée [Fr]
> An avenue or path, usually through trees or
> shrubs.

allemansrätten [Swed]
> A Swedish citizen's right to enter private land.

***Alles was geschieht, vom Grössten bis zum
Kleinsten, geschieht notwendig*** [Ger]
> Everything that happens, from the greatest to
> the least, happens of necessity: Schopenhauer's
> philosophy of life.

Alles zu seiner Zeit [Ger]
> Everything in its proper time.

allumeuse [Fr]
> A flirt; a woman who wilfully inflames male
> passions only to deny satisfaction.

Alma Mater [Lat]
> Ex-student's (***alumnus'***) school or university.

An all-purpose letter in Latin

Despite their musty image there are Latin scholars with a keen sense of humour. One of them is New Yorker Henry Beard, who offers this letter in Latin to those who wish to bemuse, confuse and delay:

Dominus meus,
Epistulam tuam accepi et rei cuius mentionem ibi
fecisti animadversionam meam promptissimam
plenissimamque dabo.
Semper vale et salve,

Which means:

Dear Sir,
I have received your letter and I will give the matter to which you referred my promptest and fullest attention.
Best wishes,

---

aloha [Haw]
> Hawaiian for hello and goodbye.

à l'outrance [Fr] (ah-loo-TRAH(N)S)
> To the bitter end.

alter ego [Lat]
> A very close and intimate friend. From the Latin meaning 'other self'.

Alte Wunden bluten leicht [Ger]
> Old wounds quickly bleed anew.

alumnus; pl. *alumni* [Lat]
> Former pupils or graduates of a school or university.

amah [Port] (AH-mah)
> Strictly speaking, a wet-nurse, but now generally used in the East to mean a nurse or maid.

amende honorable [Fr]
>A public apology for an insult.

amie [Fr]
>Mistress.

amor mio; ***mis amores*** [Sp]
>My love; my darling.

amor patriae [Lat]
>Patriotism; love of one's country.

amour [Fr] (ah-MOOR)
>A secret love affair.

amour de voyage [Fr]
>A cruise or shipboard romance.

amourette [Fr]
>A trivial love affair.

amour propre [Fr] (ah-MOOR PROP-ruh)
>Self-respect; self-esteem; inclined to vanity.

ancien régime [Fr]
>An old regime; specifically, the government of
>France before the Revolution.

anglais [Fr] (AH(N)-glay)
>English.

anglee-ya [Rus]
>England.

Anglia [Hun]
>England.

angst [Ger]
>Acute feelings of anxiety, fear and remorse,
>usually for no discernible reason.

anguis in herba [Lat]
>Snake in the grass.

an-neel [Arab]
>The Nile.

anno Domini [Lat]
>In the year of our Lord; in the Christian era.
>The date is usually preceded by the
>abbreviation AD.

anno regni [Lat]
>In the year of the reign.

annus horribilis [Lat]
> Awful year; used by Queen Elizabeth II to describe Royal fortunes in 1992.

annus mirabilis [Lat]
> Remarkable, wonderful year.

Anschluss [Ger]
> A political and economic union; specifically the annexation of Austria by Nazi Germany in 1938.

ante bellum; **antebellum** [Lat]
> The period before a war; used widely to define the period before the American Civil War.

ante meridiem [Lat]
> Before noon. Abbreviated to a.m.

antipodes [Gk]
> Those parts of the globe opposite our own; a term widely applied to Australasia.

apartheid [Afrikaans] (ah-PART-hayt)
> Former South African Government policy of racial segregation.

aperçu [Fr] (ap-er-soo)
> An insight; intuitive understanding.

apéritif [Fr]
> Alcoholic drink, often fortified wine, taken before a meal.

a posteriori [Lat] (ah-pos-teh-rih-OH-rih)
> Logical reasoning from facts and effects to cause; a principle requiring factual evidence to validate it.

apparat [Rus]
> Communist bureaucracy in the former USSR; its members and agents were ***apparatchiks***.

appliqué [Fr] (ap-PLEE-kay)
> Designs made by stitching one material upon another.

après-ski [Fr] (ap-ray-skee)
> Socializing after a day's skiing.

a priori [Lat] (ah-pree-OR-ee)
> Deductive reasoning, from cause to effect,

which without supportive observation leads to a conclusion. Such reasoning can, of course, lead to wrong conclusions.

a propos; apropos [Lat] (ap-pruh-POH)
Pertinent; with regard to; appropriate.

aquavit [Scand]
Flavoured grain or potato-based spirit.

arabesque [Fr]
In music and art, a form of complex decoration; intricate ornamentation. Also a ballet pose.

arak; arrack [Arab]
A coarse spirit distilled from rice, palm-tree sap and sugar.

à rebours [Fr]
Perversely; against the grain.

arête [Fr]
Sharp mountain ridge formed by erosion.

argot [Fr] (AH-goh)
Originally thieves' jargon; now generally used to describe any jargon.

a rivederci; arrivederci [It]
Farewell.

armoire [Fr]
Tall cupboard or wardrobe.

arrière-pensée [Fr] (ari-ayr-pah(n)-say)
An unrevealed or reserved thought; an ulterior motive.

arriviste [Fr] (ar-rih-VEEST)
Someone dedicated to ambition and determined to succeed; self-seeking.

arrondissement [Fr] (ah-roh(n)-DEES-mah(n))
Administrative subdivisions of *départements* in France; subdivisions of Paris.

ars gratia artis [Lat]
Art for art's sake.

ars longa, vita brevis [Lat]
Art is long; life is short.

à tâtons [Fr]
Tentative; groping; feeling your way.

à trois [Fr] (ah-TRWAHR)
>For three people: a meal for three; a meeting between three, etc.

attaccabottoni [It]
>A 'buttonholer'; a bore.

Auch das Schöne muss sterben [Ger]
>Even the beautiful must die (Schiller).

au contraire [Fr] (oh-kah(n)-trair)
>On the contrary.

au courant [Fr] (oh-koo-rah(n))
>Up-to-date on current affairs.

au fait [Fr] (oh-FAY)
>Fully informed.

au fond [Fr] (oh-FOR(N))
>Fundamentally; basically; essentially.

auf Wiedersehen [Ger] (ow-FVEE-duh-zayn)
>Goodbye, until we meet again.

au grand galop [Fr]
>At full gallop; at full tilt.

au gratin [Fr] (oh-grah-ta(n))
>Food covered and baked with breadcrumbs and sometimes grated cheese.

auld lang syne [Scot]
>Old times; times past.

au naturel [Fr] (oh-natch-yo-REL)
>Natural; naked.

au pair [Fr] (oh-PAIR)
>Commonly used in England to describe young people from other countries who help with housework and children in exchange for board and pocket-money.

au pied de la lettre [Fr]
>Literally; precisely. Usually abbreviated to *au pied*.

au poivre [Fr]
>Cooked with pepper.

Australian and Strine

Australian as a foreign language? Not quite.
Although faced with a plethora of outback
imagery ('I'm flat out like a lizard drinkin''),
urban crudity ('park a tiger', 'cry Ruth',
'technicolour yawn' and 300 other synonyms for
vomiting) and colourful slang ('I'm as dry as a
dead dingo's donger') we still manage to grasp
antipodean meanings without the need for
translation.

But the same can't be said of **Strine**, the very
marrow of Australian speech, delivered
primarily through the nose and partly through a
slot formed by the mouth narrow enough not to
let the flies in. **Strine** (Austreyelian = Austrine =
Strine) has its own rules, too: radical
abbreviation. Thus a 'bottle of wine' becomes a
'bolla wine'; 'Have you eaten yet?' becomes
'Jeetyet?' and 'a couple of minutes' is reduced to
'garbler mince'. Here is a small selection of
translations:

egg nisher	air conditioner
baked necks	bacon and eggs
Gunga Din, door's locked	Can't get in, door's locked
gest vonner	guest of honour
num butter buncha drongos	nothing but a bunch of drongos
top hip ride	top of the hit parade
gissa lookcha	give us a look at you
check etcher cheque yet?	Did you get your cheque yet?

au revoir [Fr] (oh-ruh-VWAHR)
>   Goodbye.

Aus den Augen, aus dem Sinn [Ger]
>   Out of sight, out of mind.

au sérieux [Fr] (oh-say-ree-UH)
>   Seriously.

Ausländer [Ger] (OW-slen-duh)
>   To Germans, an outsider or foreigner.

Autobahn [Ger]
>   German motorway.

autoestrada [Port]
>   Portuguese motorway.

autopista [Sp]
>   Spanish motorway.

autoroute [Fr]
>   French motorway.

autostrada [It]
>   Italian motorway.

autres temps, autres mœurs [Fr]
>   (oh-truh-tah(n), oh-truh-muhrs)
>   Other times, other ways: customs change with
>   the times.

avant-courier [Fr] (av-ah(n) KOOR-ih-ay)
>   A precursor; a forerunner.

avant-garde [Fr] (av-var(n)-GARD)
>   Pioneering, especially in the arts; innovative;
>   experimental.

ave atque vale [Lat]
>   Hail and farewell.

avoir du monde au balcon [Fr]
>   Expression for a well-built woman.

avoirdupois [Fr]
>   From *aver de peis* (goods of weight), the
>   system of weights (tons, hundredweights,
>   pounds and ounces) used in most English-
>   speaking countries.

avoir les cuisses légères [Fr]
>   Literally: 'to possess light thighs'; colloquial
>   expression for a woman of easy virtue.

a vuestra salud [Sp]
> Your good health.

ayah [Port]
> A maid, nurse or governess, usually to
> Europeans in Africa and the East.

B

baas [Dut]
> Boss, or employer, in some African countries.

babushka [Rus]
> A grandmother; also a headscarf worn by
> peasant women.

baccalauréat [Fr] (BAK-a-loh-ray-ah)
> French pre-university school-leaving
> examination.

bagnio [It] (BAHN-yoh)
> A brothel; also an oriental prison.

baguette [Fr] (bag-ET)
> The long French bread stick.

baignoire [Fr]
> Theatre box at stalls level.

bain-marie [Fr]
> Large pan of boiling water into which
> saucepans are placed for simmering food or
> keeping it hot.

baklava [Turk]
> Mediterranean pastry made with honey and
> nuts.

baksheesh [Pers]
> A tip or gratuity.

Don't make a boner with *baiser*

The meaning of *baiser* in some French-English dictionaries is still shown as **to kiss**, which is its correct original definiton. If a scholar were to translate a nineteenth-century novel that is exactly how it should be rendered. But . . . time has passed and now it is – most resoundingly – a French four-letter word meaning sexual activity considerably more penetrative than a kiss. *Le baiser* is therefore discouraged and you are urged to use the more prudent *embrasser*: to kiss.

ballon d'essai [Fr]
> A 'trial balloon' to test opinion.

bambino [It]
> A young child.

banco [It]
> A card gambler's offer to place a stake equal to that of the banker.

bandeau [Fr]
> A ribbon or cloth to bind a woman's hair.

banderilla [Sp]
> The dart with streamer attached that is thrust into the neck of a bull in bull-fighting. The *banderillo* is the bull-fighter who places it.

banlieue [Fr] (bah(n)-lyur)
> The suburbs.

banquette [Fr]
> Cushioned seat with a cushioned back, especially in restaurants.

banshee [Ir]
> A wailing female spirit presaging death.

bar mitzvah [Heb] (bar-MITS-vuh)
> Initiation ceremony for Jewish boys. See *bat mitzvah*.

28

barre [Fr]
> The waist-high rail around the walls of ballet school practice rooms.

bas bleu [Fr] (bah-bluhr)
> French equivalent of bluestocking: a seriously academic woman.

bateau-mouche [Fr]
> Passenger boat on the Seine around Paris.

batiste [Fr]
> Fine linen or cotton fabric.

bat mitzvah [Heb]
> Jewish girl's initiation into her religious majority at the age of twelve.

batterie de cuisine [Fr]
> A complete set of cooking utensils.

Bauhaus [Ger] (BOW-howss)
> Influential Weimar design school (1919–1933) founded by Walter Gropius.

béarnaise [Fr] (bay-uh-NAYS)
> Widely used sauce made from egg yolks, butter, vinegar and tarragon.

beatae memoriae [Lat]
> Of blessed memory.

beau geste [Fr] (boh-zhest)
> A magnanimous gesture.

beau idéal [Fr]
> An ideal of anything in beauty or excellence.

beau monde [Fr]
> The world of fashion and society.

beaux-arts [Fr] (boh-ZHAR)
> The fine arts.

beerah [Arab]
> Beer.

Beijing [Ch] (bee-ZHING)
> Formerly Peking, the Chinese capital.

bel canto [It]
> Singing in the traditional Italian manner with rich tone, perfect phrasing, clean articulation, etc.

bel esprit [Fr] (bel-es-PREE)
>Brilliant wit.

belle époque [Fr]
>The period from the late 1890s to the outbreak
>of war in 1914.

belle laide [Fr]
>A woman whose lack of beauty or irregular
>features are in themselves charming or
>attractive.

Benedictus [Lat]
>The part of the Mass that begins (in English)
>'Blessed is he that cometh in the name of the
>Lord'.

berceuse [Fr]
>A cradle song or lullaby.

bergère [Fr] (ber-ZHAIR)
>A deep, comfortable armchair.

Beschlafen Sie es [Ger]
>Sleep on it; look before you leap.

bête noire [Fr] (bayt-NWAR)
>Someone or something that is especially
>dreaded and disliked.

bêtise [Fr]
>A tactless act or remark.

Bettschwere [Ger]
>Without the energy to get out of bed.

bey [Turk]
>Governor of a Turkish town or district.

bhang [Hindi]
>Indian hemp.

bibelot [Fr] (BEEB-loh)
>Small trinket or curio.

bien entendu [Fr] (bih-yahn ah(n)-tah(n)-doo)
>Naturally; of course; understood.

bien-pensant [Fr] (bih-yahn pah(n)-sahn)
>Conformist person holding all the accepted
>opinions and beliefs.

bien trouvé [Fr] (bih-yan troo-VAY)
>A happy invention.

bijou [Fr] (BEE-zhoo)
>Small and beautiful; a trinket.

bijouterie [Fr] (bee-ZHOO-teh-ree)
>Very delicate jewellery.

billabong [Abor]
>A pool separated from the main stream of a river or creek in Australia.

billet doux [Fr] (bih-lay-DOO)
>A love-letter.

biru [Jap]
>Beer.

biretta; **birretta** [It]
>Roman Catholic clerical square cap worn by priests (black), bishops (purple), cardinals (red) and other orders (white).

bis dat qui cito dat [Lat]
>He gives twice who gives quickly: from the aphorism: 'He who gives alms to a poor man quickly, gives it twice.'

bisque [Fr] (beesk)
>Soup made from shellfish, mainly lobster.

bittertje [Dut]
>Dutch **jenever** (gin) with bitters.

blague [Fr]
>Pretentious nonsense; humbug. One who talks such nonsense or boasts is a **blagueur**.

blasé [Fr] (BLAH-zay)
>Bored indifference due to surfeit.

Blaustrumpf [Ger]
>A bluestocking. See **bas bleu**.

bleeni seekroy [Rus]
>Caviar with pancakes.

blitzkrieg [Ger]
>An intense military attack designed quickly to overwhelm the enemy.

bloembollen [Dut]
>Bulbs.

Blut ist dicker als Wasser [Ger]
>Blood is thicker than water.

Blut und Eisen [Ger]
> Blood and iron: coined by Bismarck.

Boche [Fr]
> Derogatory term for Germans.

bodega [Sp] (boh-DEG-uh)
> Wine shop.

bois [Fr] (bwah)
> Wood; ***boiserie*** is woodwork.

boîte; ***boîte de nuit*** [Fr] (bwaht de nwee)
> A disreputable club, dance-hall or dive; a nightclub.

bolas [Sp]
> Two or three heavy balls joined by cord used to entangle the legs of animals.

bollenveld [Dut]
> A bulb-field.

bombe surprise [Fr] (bom-sur-PREEZ)
> A dessert coated to hide its contents; usually ice-cream and meringue.

bonae memoriae [Lat]
> The pleasant memory of someone.

bona fide [Lat] (adj) (BOH-nuh FY-deh)
> In good faith; genuine.

bona fides [Lat] (noun)
> Good faith; honest intention.

bon appétit [Fr]
> Enjoy your meal.

bon goût [Fr] (boh(n) GOO)
> Good taste.

bon marché [Fr] (boh(n) MAR-shay)
> Cheap; also a famous bargain department store in Paris.

bon mot [Fr] (boh(n) MOH)
> A witty, clever remark.

bonne amie [Fr] (bon-ah-MEE)
> A close woman friend, who may also be more than just a friend.

bonne à tout faire [Fr] (bon-ah-too-FAIR)
> A maid-of-all-work.

bonne-bouche [Fr] (bon BOOSH)
>A tasty morsel.

bonne chance [Fr] (bon SHAH(N)S)
>Good luck!

bon ton [Fr] (boh(n) toh(n))
>Sophisticated.

bon vivant [Fr] (boh(n) vih-VAH(N))
>A person who enjoys all the luxuries but especially eating and drinking. The term **bon viveur** means the same but is not used in France.

bon voyage [Fr] (boh(n) vwah-YAHZ)
>Have a good journey!

bor [Hun]
>Wine.

bordel; **bordello** [It]
>Brothel. In French, **un bordel** is slang for a cock-up, a mess.

bordereau [Fr]
>A memorandum. The word is indelibly associated with the fake **bordereau** used to convict Dreyfus of treason.

boreh da [Welsh]
>Good morning.

borkostolo [Hun]
>Wine cellar.

borozo [Hun]
>Wine bar.

borsch; **borsh**; **borscht** [Rus]
>Vegetable and beetroot soup widely eaten in Russia and Poland.

bottega [It]
>A café and wine shop.

bouchée [Fr] (BOO-shay)
>A small pastry served hot as an hors d'œuvre.

bouclé [Fr] (BOO-klay)
>A shaggy fabric produced by looped woollen yarn.

bouffant [Fr] (BOO-fah(n))
>   Puffed-out, back-combed hair-style.

bouillabaisse [Fr] (boo-yuh-BES)
>   Provençal soup or stew of fish, vegetables and spices.

bouillon [Fr] (boo-yoh(n))
>   Thin beef or chicken broth.

Boule de Suif [Fr]
>   Literally: ball of lard – Guy de Maupassant's fictional masterpiece.

boules [Fr]
>   Game played with heavy metal balls tossed at a target ball, usually on a sand court.

bouquet garni [Fr] (boo-kay gar-nih)
>   Bunch of mixed herbs.

The *bourdalou*: why was a chamber pot named after a priest?

Although not much seen these days, except perhaps in antique shops, the small portable ladies' chamber pot known as a ***bourdalou*** poses a curious etymological puzzle. It shares its name with the celebrated seventeenth-century Jesuit preacher **Louis Bourdaloue**, but where is the connection? Were his sermons so excruciatingly long-winded?

One theory turns on the design of some early ***bourdalous***, which had eyes painted on the inside of their bottoms. Father Bourdaloue was the confessor of many of the ladies of the court whose secrets he shared; thus the symbolic all-seeing eye in a most fundamental position. A good try, but the 300-year-old secret of the ***bourdalou*** seems destined to remain a secret for another three centuries.

Bourse [Fr] (boorss)
> The French stock exchange in Paris.

Braccae tuae aperiuntur [Lat]
> Your fly is open.

brasserie [Fr]
> A restaurant that serves beer.

brioche [Fr] (bree-OSH)
> A small, sweet yeast cake.

brique [Fr]
> Slang for 10,000 francs.

brise brise [Fr]
> A net curtain for the lower half of a window.

broderie anglaise [Fr]
> Open embroidery on white cotton or fine linen.

Business bloopers

An industrial refrigeration firm once had an international sales director named C. O. Jones. He could be sent anywhere in the world except Spain and Spanish-speaking countries, where the mirth would begin at passport control and not subside until he departed. His name spelt out *cojones*, which is Spanish for testicles.

Worldwide businesses have similar problems with their products. Ford couldn't sell its Pinto in Brazil, where the name is Portuguese slang for penis. Rolls Royce couldn't understand why its Silver Mist wasn't moving in Germany until they discovered that to a German 'mist' means crap. The Finns invented a product for de-icing car doors, called it Super Piss, and are now wondering about the slow sales. The future sales prospects of a new Spanish potato crisp brand are also awaited with interest: it's called **Bum**.

---

brûle; **brûlée** [Fr]
>Flavoured with burnt sugar; also means to be 'burned' or taken advantage of.

buenas noches [Sp] (bwey-nos noh-ches)
>Good-night.

buenos dias [Sp] (bwey-nos dee-as)
>Good-day.

buffo [It] (BOO-foh)
>Burlesque; comic.

bureau à cylindre [Fr]
>A roll-top desk.

bushido [Jap]
>The feudal code of the samurai.

buvette [Fr] (boo-VET)
>Roadside café.

bwana [Swahili]
>Master; form of East African address, equivalent to 'Sir'.

C

cabaña [Sp]
>Beach hut.

cabriole [Fr]
>Type of curved furniture leg used from the eighteenth century.

cachou [Fr] (KASH-ooh)
>Breath-sweetening lozenge.

cacique [Sp]
>Originally an American Indian chief in Spanish-speaking regions; now used to mean local political boss.

cacoethes loquendi [Lat]
(kah-koh-EETH-ees loh-KWEN-dih)
An irresistible urge to talk. *Cacoethes scribendi* is a compulsive urge to write.

cadeau [Fr] (kah-doh)
A gift.

cadit quaestio [Lat]
There is nothing more to discuss.

caeteris paribus [Lat]
Other things being equal.

café [Fr] (kaff-ay)
Coffee. *Café au lait* (kaff-ay-oh-LAY) = coffee with milk; *café crème* = coffee with cream; *café noir* = black coffee.

cagoule [Fr]
Type of long anorak used by walkers.

cahier [Fr] (kay-yeh(r)
Originally a notebook; a written or printed report of a meeting or conference.

camino real [Sp]
The best way to achieve a result.

campo santo [It]
A burial ground.

canaille [Fr] (kan-EYE)
The crowd, the mob, *hoi polloi*.

canapé [Fr] (KAN-uh-pay)
Small slice of bread or toast with a savoury topping.

ça ne fait rien [Fr]
It is of no importance.

capable de tout [Fr]
Unpredictable behaviour.

capo d'opera [It]
A masterpiece.

caporal [Fr]
Type of light tobacco.

capote anglaise [Fr]
English hood, a Gallic tilt at the French letter, French slang for condom.

Caput tuum in ano est [Lat]
>An insult: you have your head up your arse.

carabiniere [It] (karah-bin-YAIR-ih)
>Armed Italian policeman.

caramba [Sp]
>A common exclamation.

caret [Lat]
>Symbol (⋀) (an insertion mark) used to indicate that something is missing in writing or printed matter.

carità pelosa [It]
>Literally: hairy generosity: generosity with some ulterior motive.

carnet [Fr] (kar-nay)
>Small booklet, usually a document.

carpe diem [Lat] (KAR-pay DEE-em)
>Make the most of today; eat, drink and be merry for tomorrow we die.

carreras de caballos [Sp]
>Horse-racing.

carretera [Sp]
>Road; highway.

carte blanche [Fr] (kart blah(n)sh)
>Having complete freedom and authority; full discretionary power.

carte-de-visite [Fr]
>Small nineteenth-century photographs on card, used as visiting cards.

carte d'identité [Fr]
>Identity card.

cartonnier [Fr]
>Cabinet with flat drawers for storing prints, drawings and plans.

cartouche [Fr]
>Inscription on an ornamental scroll.

casa [It]
>A villa or detached house.

ça saute aux yeux [Fr]
>It's obvious; it cannot be missed.

cassis [Fr]
>Blackcurrant syrup.

cassoulet [Fr]
>A meat and bean dish.

casus belli [Lat]
>An event used to justify a war or quarrel.

catachresis [Lat from Gk] (kat-uh-KREE-sis)
>The misuse of words.

catalogue raisonné [Fr] (KAT-uh-log ray-zon-ay)
>Systematic descriptive listing, usually of a collection or an artist's work.

catholicon [Gk]
>A panacea; universal remedy.

cause célèbre [Fr] (KAUZ seh-LEB-ruh)
>A famous trial, lawsuit or controversy.

causerie [Fr]
>A chatty literary essay or discussion.

ça va? [Fr] (sah-vah?)
>Everything OK?

ça va sans dire [Fr]
>That is obvious; it goes without saying.

cave [Lat] (KAH-vih)
>Slang for 'Look out!'; 'Beware!'

caveat [Lat]
>'Let him beware'. A warning or caution.

caveat emptor [Lat]
>'Let the buyer beware'; a warning that it is the buyer, not the seller, who must take the risk.

cavoli riscaldati [It]
>Literally: 'reheated cabbage'. A lapsed love affair, difficult to revive.

céad míle fáilte [Ir]
>Irish welcome: 'A hundred thousand welcomes!'

ceilidh [Gael] (KAY-lih)
>An entertainment in Scotland and Ireland, usually consisting of dancing, folk music, singing – and talking.

Cercare il pelo nell' uovo [It]
>To seek the hair in the egg; to pick faults where
>none exist.

cerveja [Port]
>Beer.

cerveza [Sp]
>Beer.

c'est la guerre [Fr] (say-lah-gair)
>That's war, it happens.

c'est la vie [Fr] (say-lah-vee)
>That's life.

ch'a [Ch]
>Tea. The British slang term is **char**.

chacun à son goût [Fr] (shah-kuh(n)-ah-soh(n)-goo)
>Everyone to their own taste.

chacun à son métier [Fr]
>(shah-kuh(n)-ah-soh(n) may-tyay)
>Everyone to their own trade.

chacun pour soi [Fr] (shah-kuh(n) poor-swahr)
>Everyone for themselves.

chagrin d'amour [Fr]
>Misery from an unhappy love affair.

chaise-longue [Fr] (shayzh-lor(ng))
>Sofa with back and one end open.

chambrer [Fr] (shahm-bray)
>To bring a red wine to room temperature.

chamise [Jap]
>Tea-house.

Changcheng [Ch]
>The Great Wall of china.

Changjiang [Ch]
>The Yangtse River.

chapati; ***chapatti*** [Hindi]
>Flat cake of unleavened bread.

charcuterie [Fr]
>Shop selling cooked meat; cold cuts of pork.

chargé d'affaires [Fr] (shar-zhay da-FAIR)
>Diplomatic representative below the rank of
>ambassador.

charivari [Fr]
>A demonstrative racket or celebration.

charpoy [Urdu]
>Indian bed, usually of woven hemp.

chasse [Fr] (shas)
>A liqueur following coffee.

chat; ***chatte*** [Fr]
>*Chat* and *chatte* may be *cat* but they're also slang terms for *pussy*.

Châteaubriand [Fr] (shah-toh-brih-ah(n))
>Thick steak cut from a fillet of beef.

chaud-froid [Fr] (shoh-frwah)
>Cold meat or chicken covered with a savoury jellied sauce.

chef de mission [Fr]
>Organizer or leader of a team.

chef d'équipe [Fr]
>Manager of a team.

chef-d'œuvre [Fr] (shef DURV-ruh)
>A masterpiece.

chemin de fer [Fr]
>A game of cards like baccarat.

cheongsam [Ch]
>A long straight oriental dress with a high collar and a slit on one side of the skirt.

cherchez la femme [Fr] (shair-shay-luh-fahm)
>'Look for the woman'; there's always a woman involved.

chère amie [Fr] (shair ah-mee)
>A mistress or sweetheart.

chéri(e) [Fr] (sheh-ree)
>Darling.

che sarà sarà [It] (kay-suh-RAH-suh-RAH)
>What will be, will be.

chevaux de frise [Fr]
>Iron spikes or some other sharp deterrent on the tops of fences and walls.

chez [Fr] (shay)
>At the house of – e.g.: *Chez Humperdinck*.

chez moi [Fr] (shay mwah)
    At my house.
chez nous [Fr] (shay noo)
    At our house.
chiasse [Fr]
    Slang term for 'the runs' induced by fear.

The challenge of Chinese

Chinese is the language of one billion people, and is thus the most-used language in the world. But many of those billion users can't understand one another; while written Chinese is standard, spoken Chinese comes in many varieties which are mutually unintelligible. The main and official dialect is Mandarin but huge numbers of the population (plus Hong Kong and Singapore Chinese) speak Cantonese.

The written language remains a closed book to most westerners but the notion of phonetically spelling out Chinese with Roman characters – called **Pinyin** – has helped to make the spoken language more accessible. Well, somewhat accessible: if you manage to master the pronunciation system of **Pinyin** you are then faced with the four tones – for spoken Chinese is above all a tonal language. The character *ma*, if spoken with the first tone, means 'mother'; the same character spoken with the third tone means 'horse'. If you intend to tackle Chinese, be prepared for glorious confusion!

You will also have noticed that many spellings, particularly of place-names, have changed in recent years so that they read roughly how they sound in Mandarin: Peking to **Beijing**; Mao Tse-tung to **Mao Zedong**, Canton to **Guangzhou**, China to **Zhóngghuó**, and so on.

Chi bestia va a Roma bestia ritorna [It]
>He that goes to Rome a fool returns a fool.

chicane [Fr]
>Sharp, narrow bends on a motor racing circuit.

chignon [Fr] (SHEE-nyor(n))
>The roll or coil of hair at the back of a woman's head.

chikatet [Jap]
>Japanese underground railway systems.

chin-chin; *ch'ing ch'ing* [Ch]
>Informal greeting, farewell or toast.

chronique scandaleuse [Fr]
>A scandalous story or gossip.

chun jie [Ch]
>Chinese New Year.

chutzpah [Yid]
>Shameless audacity; cheek.

ciao [It] (chow)
>Hullo; goodbye.

cicerone [It]
>   (chih-chuh-ROH-nih, or sih-suh-ROH-nih)
>A guide, especially at sites of antiquities.

ci-devant [Fr]
>Former; that used to be; quondam.

cinquecento [It] (ching-kweh-CHEN-toh)
>The period from 1500 to 1600.

circa [Lat] (SER-kuh)
>Approximately; at the approximate time of. Abbreviated to **c** or **ca** and used before a date: **c1990**.

ciré [Fr] (see-ray)
>Smooth, usually waxed, fabric.

clachan [Gael]
>Small rural village in Scottish West Highlands.

claque [Fr] (klak)
>Originally a group hired to applaud in a theatre; now used in a derogatory way to describe a group of sycophants blindly applauding their leader. Such people are *claqueurs*.

cocotte [Fr]
>   Prostitute; also a fireproof cooling dish.

coitus interruptus [Lat]
>   Interruption or avoidance of orgasm, by with-
>   drawal during sexual intercourse. In Australia
>   it is called 'Getting off at Redfern' (the station
>   just before the terminus, Sydney Central).

Comédie Française [Fr]
>   The French national theatre in Paris.

comédie humaine [Fr] (kom-uh-dee ooh-mayn)
>   The comedy of life. *La Comédie Humaine* is
>   the title of Balzac's fictional social history of
>   France.

comédie noire [Fr] (kom-uh-dee nwahr)
>   Black comedy.

comme ci, comme ça [Fr]
>   Neither good nor bad.

commedia dell'arte [It] (kom-ay-dyah del-ah-tay)
>   The well-known characters of Columbine,
>   Harlequin and Punchinello are from this
>   stylized Italian comedy genre established in the
>   sixteenth century.

comme il faut [Fr] (kom-eel-foh)
>   Correct; in accordance with acceptable
>   manners.

commère [Fr]
>   A female *compère*.

commis [Fr] (com-mih)
>   An assistant or apprentice waiter or chef.

commune [Fr]
>   The smallest administrative division in France
>   (also in Belgium, Switzerland and Italy),
>   governed by a mayor and council.

compère [Fr]
>   The host or commentator of an entertainment,
>   contest or programme. See *commère*.

compos mentis [Lat]
>   Sane; of sound mind. See *non compos
>   mentis*.

con amore [It]
> To be performed lovingly.

con brio [It]
> With energy; to be performed with spirit.

concours d'élégance [Fr]
> (koh(n)-koor day-lay-gah(n)s)
> Beauty parade of vintage, veteran or exotic motor cars.

confrère [Fr] (ko(n)-frair)
> A professional colleague.

connard [Fr]
> Extremely rude expression for a fool, an idiot, someone stupid or dumb.

consommé [Fr] (kohn-SOH-may)
> Clear meat or chicken soup.

contra mundum [Lat]
> Against the world; in the face of accepted wisdom.

contrat social [Fr] (kor(n)-trah soh-seeal)
> The surrender of certain personal liberties to the community in return for an organized society.

coq au vin [Fr] (kok oh vah(n))
> Chicken cooked in red wine.

coquilles St Jacques [Fr] (koh-khee sah(n) zhahk)
> Seafood cooked in sauces and served in scallop shell.

coram populo [Lat]
> In full view of the people; in public.

cordon bleu [Fr] (kor-doh(n) blehr)
> First class, especially applied to cooking and chefs.

corniche [Fr] (kor-NEESH)
> Coastal road, typically cut into steep mountains. The road between Nice and Monte Carlo is a famous example.

cornuto [It]
> Literally: 'horned'. A male insult to another, implying he has been cuckolded.

Corpus Christi [Lat]
> The festival of the Blessed Sacrament or Holy Eucharist.

corpus delicti [Lat]
> The sum of the facts that constitute an offence in law. Often incorrectly used to describe the corpse or body in connection with a crime.

corrida; ***corrida de toros*** [Sp]
> Bull-fight; the running of bulls.

corroboree [Aust Abor] (koh-ROB-uh-ree)
> Australian aboriginal dance ceremony.

cortège [Fr] (kor-tehzh)
> A procession, especially one following a funeral.

Cosa Nostra [It]
> US branch of the Sicilian mafia organization.

Così fan tutte, ossia La Scuola degli amanti [It]
> All women do it; that is the way of all women. Mozart's opera.

Côte d'Azur [Fr] (koht dah-ZOOR)
> The French Riviera.

Côte de Beaune [Fr] (koht duh-BONE)
> Southern part of the Côte d'Or wine-growing region of France, from Beaune to Santenay.

Côte de Nuits [Fr] (koht duh NWEE)
> Northern part of the Côte d'Or Burgundy region from Dijon to Nuits-St-Georges.

Côte d'Or [Fr] (koht dor)
> The Burgundy region of France, 300 km south-east of Paris.

côtelette [Fr]
> A chop or cutlet.

couilles [Fr]
> Testicles. Used commonly and vulgarly and with infinite variety. ***Mes couilles!*** = bollocks.

coulant [Fr]
> Easy-going; easy to get on with.

couleur du temps [Fr]
> Whichever way the wind blows; according to circumstances.

Countries, cities and place-names

For a century and a half the British have freely
anglicized foreign place-names, often in defiance
of the spelling and pronunciation used by the
natives. If you asked a citizen of Beijing (we've
perversely called it Peking for generations) if you
were in China you'd be met with an
uncomprehending stare; there the country is
called **Zhōngghuó**. We say Athens and Corfu;
the Greeks say – and they should know – **Athena**
and **Kerkira**. The country we know as Sweden
is really **Sverige**; Brussels is **Bruxelles**; Italy is
Italia; Hungary is **Magyarország** where, to be
fair, they call Great Britain **Nagy-Britannia**.

But, slowly, English speakers are becoming
more internationalized, and many of us can now
work out that **Firenze** is Florence, **Köpenhamn**
is Copenhagen and **München** is Munich.

coup de foudre [Fr] (koo duh food-ruh)
> Love at first sight; a sudden and surprising
> event.

coup de grâce [Fr] (koo duh grahs)
> A final or decisive stroke; a mortal blow that
> ends a victim's suffering.

coup de main [Fr] (koo du ma(n))
> A surprise attack.

coup d'essai [Fr] (koo day-say)
> A trial or first attempt.

coup d'état [Fr] (koo day-tah)
> A violent seizure of power, usually the illegal
> overturning of a government.

coup de théâtre [Fr] (koo duh teh-art-ruh)
> A sudden and dramatic action; a sensational
> stage success.

coup d'œil [Fr] (koo DUH-ee)
> A quick glimpse.

coureur [Fr]
>A skirt-chaser; a womanizer.

couscous [Fr from Arab *kouskous*] (koos-koos)
>Spicy North African dish of steamed flour paste served with stew.

coûte que coûte [Fr] (koot kuh koot)
>No matter what the cost; at all costs.

couvert [Fr]
>A set place at a meal table; a restaurant 'cover' for which a charge is made.

craquelure [Fr]
>Crazing on the surface of old oil paintings and on pottery glazing.

crème de la crème [Fr] (krem-du-lah-krem)
>Cream of the cream; the very best.

cri de cœur [Fr] (krih duh kur)
>A cry from the heart.

crime passionnel [Fr] (kreem pass-yuh-NEL)
>A crime motivated by the passions: often murder, usually sexual passion.

crise de conscience [Fr]
>An attack of moral doubt; an awakening of one's scruples.

crise de cœur [Fr]
>An emotional crisis; a catastrophic love affair.

crise de nerfs [Fr] (krees duh nairf)
>An hysterical attack; a brief nervous breakdown.

Croix de Guerre [Fr] (krwah duh gair)
>French militay decoration for gallantry first awarded in 1915.

croûte [Fr] (kroot)
>Crust; fried bread used as a base for savouries.

croûtons [Fr] (kroo-toh(n))
>Cubes of toasted or fried bread usually served in soup.

crudités [Fr] (kroo-dih-tay)
>Appetizer of sliced, raw mixed vegetables served with dips or sauces.

csarda [Hung] (char-duh)
> A country inn.

csárdás [Hung]
> Hungarian national dance.

cuentaselo a tu abuela [Sp]
> Tell that to your grandmother!

cui bono? [Lat] (kwee boh-noh)
> For whose benefit? Who will profit by it?

cui malo? [Lat] (kwee mah-loh)
> Whom will it harm?

cum grano salis [Lat]
> With a grain of salt; not to be taken literally; treat with caution.

cum laude [Lat] (kum LOW-day)
> With praise; an above-average examination pass; a pass with distinction. (See also *magna cum laude*.)

curé [Fr] (kyoor-ray)
> French parish priest.

currente calamo [Lat]
> Writing that's dashed off without pause.

curriculum vitae [Lat]
> Abbreviation *CV*. An outline of someone's educational and professional history, usually submitted with a job application.

cwm [Welsh] (koom)
> A valley.

Cymraeg; *Cymric* [Welsh]
> The Welsh language.

Cymru [Welsh]
> Wales

D

dacha [Rus] (DAH-tshuh)
>Russian country house or villa.

Dáil [Ir] (doyl)
>Parliament of the Irish Republic in Dublin.

damnosa hereditas [Lat]
>A disastrous inheritance; one that brings
>problems rather than benefits.

da multos annos [Lat]
>A wish for someone's long life.

Danish and *Nudansk*

Danish, or one of the many versions of it like
Nudansk ('new Danish'), is spoken by five
million Danes, many of whom are on excellent
terms with English. But their own language,
developed over a millennium, is idiosyncratically
colourful. Here are a couple of samples; there
are no prizes for identifying the English versions
of these two famous lines, both linked to a
Shakespearian brush with Denmark four
centuries ago:

- *Der er noget råddent i Danmarks rige.*
- *Lykken er en cigar, der hedder Hamlet.*

Courtesy Oxford University Press Dictionaries.

Answers on page 52

danse du ventre [Fr]
> Variety of belly dancing.

danse macabre [Fr] (dah(n)s muh-KARB-ruh)
> The dance of death.

Darunter und darüber [Ger]
> Topsy-turvy.

Das fragt sich [Ger]
> That remains to be seen.

Das kleinste Haar wirft seinen Schatten [Ger]
> The smallest hair casts a shadow. Attributed to
> Goethe.

de bene esse [Lat]
> Subject to certain conditions; without
> prejudice; provisionally.

déboutonné; déboutonnée [Fr]
> Unbuttoned; careless; sloppy.

déclassé [Fr] (day-klas-say)
> Having lost one's social status.

décolletage [Fr] (day-kol-TAHZH)
> A revealing low-cut neckline on a woman's
> dress. ***Décolleté*** is the act of wearing such a
> neckline.

de die in diem [Lat]
> From day to day.

de facto [Lat] (day FAK-toh)
> In reality; in fact.

défense d'entrer [Fr] (dah-fah(n)s dah(n)-tray)
> No entry.

défense de fumer [Fr] (dah-fah(n)s duh-foo-may)
> No smoking.

dégagé [Fr] (day-gah-zhay)
> Relaxed; unconstrained; detached.

dégueulasse [Fr]
> Repugnant. Used vulgarly: ***c'est un***
> ***dégueulasse!*** = he's a rotten sod.

de gustibus (non est disputandum) [Lat]
> There's no accounting for tastes.

de haut en bas [Fr] (duh-oh-ah(n) bah)
> Consciously superior; in a condescending way.

Dei gratia [Lat]
>By the grace of God.

déjà vu [Fr]
>The feeling or conviction that an experience is being repeated: a journey, a place revisited, an event, etc.

delineavit; del [Lat]
>(He/she) drew it. Used with the name of the artist: Hogarth ***del***.

Danish Answers

The two lines, translated, are: 'Something is rotten in the state of Denmark, and 'Happiness is a cigar called Hamlet.'

---

delirium tremens [Lat]
>Slang: the dt's. Psychotic condition exhibiting delirium, tremor and hallucinations, induced by excessive intake of alcohol.

démarche [Fr] (day-mahsh)
>A new move in political or diplomatic affairs.

demi-mondaine [Fr]
>A woman of the ***demi-monde***, of low repute.

demi-tasse [Fr]
>A small coffee cup; a small cup of coffee.

démon de midi [Fr]
>Reawakening of sexual appetite in middle-age.

de mortuis (nil nisi bonum) [Lat]
>Say nothing bad about the dead.

de nos jours [Fr] (duh noh zhoor)
>Of our time. Used after a name: 'She was the George Sand ***de nos jours***.'

dénouement [Fr] (day-NOO-moh(n))
>The unravelling of a mystery and its solution.

Deo Optimo Maximo [Lat]
> To God the greatest. Motto of the Benedictine order; the initials DOM are seen on the labels of Benedictine liqueur.

Deo volente; abbrev. ***DV*** [Lat]
> God willing; unless something prevents it.

de profundis [Lat]
> (A cry) from the depths of despair. The first two words of the Latin version of Psalm 130 and the title of Oscar Wilde's apologia published in 1905.

député [Fr] (day-puh-tay)
> Member of the French lower house of parliament.

dérailler [Fr]
> Slang for 'to go off the rails'.

de règle [Fr] (duh REHG-luh)
> Required by rule or convention.

Der ewige Jude [Ger]
> The eternal Jew.

de rigueur [Fr] (duh-rih-GOOR)
> Required by etiquette.

dernier cri [Fr] (der-nyay kree)
> Latest fashion; trendy.

dernier ressort [Fr]
> A last resort.

derrière [Fr]
> Buttocks.

Der Schuster hat die schlechtesten Schuhe [Ger]
> The shoemaker has the worst shoes.

déshabillé [Fr] (day-zhuh-bee-yay)
> In a state of undress; a dressing-gown.

détente [Fr] (day-TAH(N)T)
> Relaxation of a state of tension, usually between two countries.

détraqué [Fr]
> Unbalanced; insane; out of order.

deus ex machina [Lat] (DAY-uhs eks MAK-ee-nuh)
> A god or unlikely character who appears, in a

53

play or novel, to solve the mystery or resolve the plot.

Deus vobiscum [Lat]

God be with you.

Deuxième Bureau [Fr]

French counterpart of Britain's MI5, the Military Intelligence Department.

dharma [Hindi]

Social custom that is religious and moral duty in Hinduism. For Buddhists it is the truth as taught by Buddha.

dharna [Hindi]

The practice of obtaining justice by sitting or fasting on the doorstep of the home of the offender.

dhobi [Hindi]

A washerman or washerwoman in India.

dhoti [Hindi]

Male loincloth as worn in India.

dialogue des sourds [Fr]

Discussion in which neither party listens to the other.

Diaspora [Gk]

The dispersion of the Jews from ancient Palestine 597–538 BC.

Dieu et mon droit [Fr] (DYU ay mo(n) DRWUH)

God and my right. The motto of the Royal Arms of Great Britain.

Directoire [Fr] (dih-rek-TWHAR)

The fashions of the French Directory period, 1795–9, following classical lines which in turn inspired English Regency fashions.

dirndl [Ger] (durn-duhl)

Alpine peasant-style dress with full gathered skirt, tight waist and bodice, and blouse with short puffed sleeves.

dis aliter visum [Lat]

The gods decided otherwise.

disjecta membra [Lat]
> Scattered fragments of a writer's literary work.

distingué [Fr] (dees-TAH(N)-gay)
> Distinguished in manner and appearance.

djellabah *see also* ***jellaba*** [Arab]
> Hooded cloak with wide sleeves worn in North Africa.

djibbah [Arab]
> Long open coat worn by Muslims.

djinn [Arab]
> Spirit in Muslim mythology able to assume human and animal form. Sometimes spelt ***jinnee, jinni***.

dolce far niente [It]
> Relaxed idleness.

dolce vita [It] (DOL-chay VEE-tah)
> Life of luxury and sensuality.

dolmathes; dolmades [Gk]
> Traditional Greek dish of vine leaves stuffed with savoury rice.

Dominus illuminatio mea [Lat]
> The Lord is my light. Motto of Oxford University.

Donner und Blitz [Ger]
> Thunder and lightning. An expression of amazement.

doppelgänger [Ger]
> An apparition identical to a living person.

douane [Fr] (doo-AH(N))
> Customs office.

douanier [Fr] (doo-AH(N)-yay)
> Customs officer.

double entendre [Fr] (doo-blah(n)-TAH(N)-druh)
> A word or phrase having two interpretations, one of them indelicate. The phrase ***double entente*** is used in France and means the same.

Drachenfutter [Ger]
> Literally: 'dragonfodder'. A guilty husband's present to his wife.

droit de cité [Fr]
> Freedom of a city, club or organization.

droit de seigneur [Fr]
> In feudal times, the right of a lord to sleep with his tenant's bride on her wedding night.

Duae tabulae rasae in quibus nihil scriptum est [Lat]
> 'Two minds without a single thought' – the motto of movie comedians Laurel and Hardy.

d'un certain age [Fr]
> A woman of unspecified middle-age.

Dutch dung

British tourists in Holland are often taken aback by the wide and frequent use there of the expletive **shit**. The word was borrowed from English but to the Dutch it is the mildest of epithets and as meaningless as **gee, blimey** or **gosh**. It's a phenomenon of language borrowing that a word weighed down with vulgarity in one country may be merely an amusing trifle in another. A century or so ago the English borrowed such a word from the Dutch. We know it as **poppycock**; they know it as ***pappekak***, which means 'soft shit'.

---

dydda [Welsh]
> Good day!

E

eau-de-nil [Fr] (oh-duh-nil)
  A tint of pale green.

eau-de-vie [Fr]
  Literally: 'Water of life'; but it is in fact a rough brandy.

ébauche [Fr] (ay-bohsh)
  A writer's rough outline for a novel; a quick sketch.

Ecce Homo [Lat] (ek-ee hoh-moh)
  The image of Christ crowned with thorns.

ecce lacunar mirum! [Lat]
  'Now, that's a ceiling!' to be murmured approvingly in the Sistine Chapel.

echt [Ger]
  Genuine; pure; unadulterated.

éclair [Fr]
  A chocolate-covered, cream-filled small pastry.

éclaircissement [Fr] (ay-klair-sis-mah(n))
  A revelation; an explanation.

éclat [Fr] (ay-KLAH)
  A great success; a dazzling effect.

école [Fr] (ay-KOHL)
  A school; a group of artistic disciples.

écrasse! [Fr]
  Shut up!

écritoire [Fr] (ay-krih-TWAHR)
  Writing desk. Escritoire is still widely used in Britain.

57

écru [Fr] (ay-kroo)
> Greyish-yellow: the colour of unbleached linen.

écurie [Fr] (ay-kyoo-REE)
> A works motor racing team.

Edelweiss [Ger]
> Small white Alpine flowering plant.

eekra [Rus]
> Caviar.

Effendi [Turk]
> An important person; a gentleman.

egeszsegeunkre! [Hung]
> Cheers!

Egri Bikaver [Hung]
> Bull's Blood red wine.

Eine Schwalbe macht keinen Sommer [Ger]
> One swallow doesn't make a summer.

Ein unnütz Leben ist ein früher Tod [Ger]
> A wasted life is premature death (Goethe).

Eisen und Blut [Ger]
> Iron and blood.

élan [Fr] (ay-lah(n))
> Vivacity; style and vigour.

Elatha [Gk]
> Greece.

eldorado; *El Dorado* [Sp]
> A place of fabled opportunity; the fabled South American city of immense riches.

elinikos kafes [Gk]
> Greek coffee.

embarras de choix [Fr]
> So many options it's difficult to make a choice.

embarras de richesses [Fr]
> Embarrassment of riches; so many options to choose from.

embonpoint [Fr] (ah(n)-bor(n)-pwah(n))
> Attractive plumpness.

embouchure [Fr] (arh(m)-boo-SHOOR)
> The correct placing of the lips and tongue when playing a brass instrument.

emeritus [Lat]

> Retired, but retaining the title, often on an honorary basis. Usually, an emeritus professor.

éminence grise [Fr] (ah-min-ah(n)s-GREEZ)

> Literally: 'grey eminence'. Someone who wields considerable power behind the scenes.

empressement [Fr]

> Enthusiastic display of cordiality.

en avant [Fr] (ah(n) ah-VAH(N))

> Move ahead! Forward!

en bloc [Fr] (ah(n)-BLOK)

> In a body; all together.

en brochette [Fr]

> Food grilled on a skewer.

en brosse [Fr] (ah(n) BROS)

> Hair cut short and bristly. In Britain, known as the 'bog-brush' style.

enceinte [Fr] (ah(n)-SAY(N)T)

> Pregnant.

enchiridion [Gk]

> A handbook; manual, work of reference.

endimanché [Fr]

> Dressed in Sunday best.

en famille [Fr] (ah(n) fah-MEE-uh)

> As one of the family; informal.

enfant chérie [Fr]

> A favourite, pampered child.

enfant gâté [Fr]

> A spoiled child; an adult who behaves like a spoiled child.

enfant terrible [Fr] (ah(n)-fah(n) teh-REEB-luh)

> Someone who embarrasses by being unconventional, indiscreet, opinionated and loud.

en fête [Fr]

> In festive mood.

en l'air [Fr]

> Up in the air; vague; left for discussion.

59

English found wanting

Here's a letter to *The Times* complaining about the elitist use of foreign words in the paper:

'Sir, Your leading article of November 30 tells us that "The attitude of '*L'etat, c'est moi*' is an affliction that comes . . ."

'Some of your readers would not know what this means.

'I am one of them and I have been reading your newspaper for over 30 years. Of course, I can guess fairly accurately; I have seen the phrase before and having looked it up in the back of my dictionary, find that I was just about right.

'Even [Bernard] Levin, for a change, managed to get through an article on the opposite page without resorting to bits of Latin, etc, in italics. I wonder if all your own staff can unhesitatingly read through these foreign phrases and know what they mean better than if they were written in English.

'I don't share John Major's wish for a classless society, but as they are, your articles are for that

en öl [Swed] (an erl)
   Beer.
en passant [Fr] (ah(n) pas-SAH(N))
   In passing; a chess move for capturing a pawn.
en paz descanse [Sp]
   May he rest in peace.
en pension [Fr]
   Living in lodgings as a boarder.
en plein air [Fr] (ah(n) plah(n)air)
   In the open air.
en plus [Fr] (ah(n) ploos)
   In addition.

class of people who were taught French, Latin or whatever language you decide to make use of.'

The letter ran without editorial comment, but a week later another reader replied:

'Sir, (The letter of December 3) highlights the prejudices that many people still maintain towards foreign languages. There are certain phrases which in their source language are far more graphic, concise and eloquent than if they are translated.

'Are we to emasculate our language to such a point that any phrases which might be considered difficult or elitist should be banned? Why stop at foreign phrases? We would soon be at a nadir of linguistic expression unmatched even by Enid Blyton.

'The richness of any language develops from its history and its contact with other countries and their language and literature. It is high time that we all realise this.'

en principe [Fr]
> A very common colloquial expression roughly meaning 'in theory' or 'as a rule' but conveying a strong note of scepticism.

en rapport [Fr] (ah(n) rah-por)
> In sympathy; in harmony.

en revanche [Fr]
> In return; as an act of retaliation.

entente cordiale [Fr]
> (ah(n)-TAH(N)T kor-DYAHL)
> A friendly understanding between countries.

en-tout-cas [Fr] (ah(n) too-kar)
> An umbrella-style sunshade.

entr'acte [Fr] (ah(n)-trak)
>Interval between theatrical acts.

entrecôte [Fr]
>Tenderloin or rib steak.

entre deux guerres [Fr]
>The period between World War I and World War II.

Entre-Deux-Mers [Fr] (Ah(n)-truh dur Mair)
>Large wine area of the Gironde, between the Dordogne and Garonne rivers.

entre la espada y la pared [Sp]
>Literally: between the sword and the wall. Means 'between the devil and the deep blue sea'.

entremets [Fr] (ah(n)-tru-may)
>Side dish served between main courses of a meal.

entre nous [Fr]
>Between ourselves; in strict confidence.

entrepôt [Fr] (ah(n)-truh-pot)
>A commercial warehouse; a trading centre or port.

en un clin d'oeil [Fr]
>In the twinkling of an eye.

en villégiature [Fr]
>Holidaying or staying in the country.

épatant [Fr] (ay-pah-tah(n))
>Astounding; mind-boggling.

e pluribus unum [Lat]
>One out of many. The motto of USA.

épris [Fr]
>In love; enamoured.

è pur troppo vero [It]
>It is only too true.

eretz ha-kodesh [Heb]
>Holy Land.

ergo [Lat]
>Therefore; hence.

Er hat Bohnen in den Ohren [Ger]
>He has beans in his ears; none are so deaf as those who will not listen.

Er hat Haare auf den Zähnen [Ger]
>He has hairs on his teeth; he is a sharp one.

Erin go bragh; ***Eire go brath*** [Ir]
>Ireland forever!

ersatz [Ger]
>A poor imitation; an inferior substitute.

erwtensoep [Dut]
>Favourite Dutch dish of thick pea soup with smoked sausage, pork fat and pig's knuckle.

escándalo [Sp]
>A scandal, a fuss.

escargot [Fr] (es-kar-goh)
>Edible snails.

Es fällt keine Eiche von einem Streiche [Ger]
>You can't fell an oak with a single stroke.

Es ist nicht alles Gold, was glänzt [Ger]
>All is not gold that glitters.

eso una tramp [Sp]
>It's a fix! Often shouted at sporting events.

espadrille [Fr] (es-pah-dreel)
>Casual rope-soled canvas shoe.

esprit de corps [Fr]
>Pride in belonging to a group; a shared sense of fellowship, loyalty and purpose.

esprit de l'escalier [Fr] (es-pree duh les-KAHL-yay)
>The brilliant remark that one thinks of too late.

esprit fort [Fr] (es-pree FOR)
>An independent thinker.

es regnet in Strömen [Ger]
>It's pouring with rain.

Es stirbt als Knabe, wen die Götter lieben [Ger]
>Those whom the gods love die young.

estaminet [Fr] (es-tah-mee-nay)
>Small bar.

est deus in nobis [Lat]
>There is a god within us. (Ovid)

estiatorion [Gk]

>   In Greece, an ordinary restaurant.

étagère [Fr]

>   Hanging set of shelves or bookshelves.

et alii [Lat]

>   And others; and other things. Abbreviation =
>   ***et al.***

état d'âme [Fr]

>   The state of the soul; how a person feels deep
>   down.

et cetera; ***etc.*** [Lat]

>   And so on; and the rest.

étoile [Fr] (ay-TWAHL)

>   Star-shaped.

être cousu d'argent [Fr]

>   To be rolling in money.

et sequentia; ***et seq.*** [Lat]

>   And the following.

et tu, Brute! [Lat] (et-TOO, BROO-tay)

>   Allegedy Julius Caesar's last words when he saw
>   Brutus among his assassins. Used ever since
>   to reproach a friend who betrays.

étude [Fr] (ay-TOOD)

>   A short musical composition to highlight the
>   technical virtuosity of a soloist.

eureka [Gk]

>   'I have found it!' said Archimedes upon
>   discovering the principle of specific gravity.
>   Now used as an expression of delight in finding
>   the answer to a problem.

Europäische Wirtschafts Gemeinschaft [Ger]

>   European Community.

Europäische Union [Ger]

>   European Union.

événement [Fr]

>   Event, occurrence, result; climax.

Ewigkeit [Ger]

>   Thin air; eternity; the unknown.

Eurospeak

When **discothèque** crossed the Channel it seemed an innocent enough borrowing. The French certainly didn't mind, but they did mind what they received in return: an unstoppable and unquenchable youthspeak – a rock and pop jargon that has, over the past three decades, travelled to the far frontiers of Europe, where the French relax on *un living* (living room furniture) and wish each other *Bon weekend!*, Russians kick off their *shoozy* and play *diskis*, Italians listen to their *rockmen* and *long playings* while the Germans go out *joggen*.

English has for some time been Europe's preferred second language. Most Danes speak it fluently, as do large numbers of Dutch and Belgians; 80% of French and German secondary pupils study it. But that's English in its proper European place; what is less welcome is the infiltration of unnecessary, inappropriate, bastardized and often meaningless English words and phrases into the various European languages to create *franglais* (*see article, page* 74), *Itangliano*, **Swinglish** and other hybrids. As *Pravda* once gravely reported, the phenomenon was a *seriosnaya situasia* and a *nationalnaya problema*.

ex cathedra [Lat]
  With unquestioned authority; infallible.
exceptis excipiendis [Lat]
  When the appropriate exceptions have been made.
exempli gratia; *e.g.* [Lat]
  For example.

exeunt [Lat]
> A stage direction meaning 'leaves the stage' or 'go out'.

ex granis fit acervus [Lat]
> Many grains make a heap; every little helps.

ex gratia [Lat] (eks GRAY-shuh)
> A payment made as a favour, not by legal right.

ex libris [Lat]
> From the library of. Usually seen on bookplates.

ex nihilo nihil fit [Lat]
> Nothing produces nothing.

ex officio [Lat]
> By virtue of one's office.

ex ore parvulorum veritas [Lat]
> Out of the mouths of babes comes truth.

ex parte [Lat] (ex PART-ih)
> In law, in the interests of one party only; a temporary injunction granted to one party in the absence of the other.

extrait [Fr]
> A copy of a certificate; an extract: ***extrait de naissance*** = birth certificate; ***extrait mortuaire*** = death certificate.

extraordinaire [Fr]
> Extraordinary; exceptional.

F

fabbrica [It]
> Factory.

faber est quisque fortunae suae [Lat]
> We are all architects of our fortunes.

façade d'honneur [Fr]
> The main frontage of a building.

facile largire de alieno [Lat]
> It is easy to be generous with what is another's.

facile princeps [Lat] (fas-ih-lih PRIN-seps)
> Easily the best; the acknowledged leader.

façon de parler [Fr]
> Way of speaking; mere words, all effect and no sincerity.

facta non verba [Lat]
> Deeds, not words.

factotum [Lat]
> A jack-of-all-trades.

fac ut gaudeam [Lat]
> Make my day.

fadastikos! [Gk]
> Fantastic!

fahrt [Ger]
> Ubiquitous word important to car drivers:
> ***Durchfahrt verboten*** = No entry; ***Ausfahrt*** = Exit; ***Einfahrt frei halten*** = Do not block entrance, etc.

faire l'amende honorable [Fr]
> To apologize; to make amends.

faire la sourde oreille [Fr]
> To turn a deaf ear.

faire ses choux gras [Fr]
> To fatten your cabbages; to feather your nest.

fait accompli [Fr] (fet ah-KOM-plee)
> An accomplished fact; something already done.

faits divers [Fr]
> Short news items; news in brief.

faites vos jeux [Fr] (fet voh ZHUR)
> Place your bets.

falafel [Heb]
> Fried chick-peas served in pitta bread.

False friends

They're called **des Faux Amis**, dangerous duos, treacherous twins, **Mots-Pièges**, false friends. And with good reason: they are words of a foreign language that so closely resemble English words that we are led to believe they share the same meaning. On the contrary: many have completely different meanings, and howlers inevitably result when the user is unaware of the difference. Here is just a small selection:

French false friends

Agenda: note book, diary. **Apprécier**: estimate. **Commodité**: comfort, convenience. **Delayer**: to dilute, to water down. **Demander**: sometimes to demand but also a mild request, or to wonder. **Éventuel**: possible. **Lunatique**: capricious, fickle. **Pet**: fart. **Prétendre**: to assert, to claim. **Supplier**: beseech. **User**: to wear out (**Cela s'use vite**: it wears out quickly).

German false friends

Bald: soon. **Chef**: boss, manager. **Fast**: almost,

---

farce est jouée (la) [Fr]
> 'The comedy is over' – supposedly the death-bed utterance of Rabelais.

farceur [Fr] (far-SUR)
> A wag or practical joker; a writer of stage farces.

fasullo [It]
> False, fake.

fata morgana [It] (far-tuh mor-GAR-nuh)
> Originally a mirage seen in the Straits of Messina; now any mirage or similar illusion.

nearly. *Fatal*: annoying. *Fix*: quick, smart.
Genial: brilliant, gifted, brainy. *Kaution*:
guarantee, deposit. *Gift*: poison. *Slip*: knickers.
Spenden: to give, to donate.

Italian false friends
Accidenti: damn! *Camera*: room. *Confetti*:
sugar-coated almonds. *Lunatico*: moody.
Magazzino: storehouse. *Parente*: a relation.
Promiscuo: mixed. *Rumore*: noise.
Sofisticato: adulterated. *Suggestivo*: striking,
picturesque. *Superbo*: arrogant.

Spanish false friends
Advertir: to give warning. *Carpeta*: office file.
Constipados: suffering from a cold.
Extenuar: to weaken. *Injuria*: insult.
Intoxicado: not drunk, but poisoned.
Particular: private, personal. *Suceso*: an event,
Happening.*tormenta*: storm. *Voluble*:
changeable.

faubourg [Fr] (foh-boorg)
> An inner suburb, usually a working-class
> neighbourhood.
fausse dévote [Fr]
> Pious hypocrite.
faute de mieux [Fr] (foht duh MYUR)
> For want of something better.
faux bonhomme [Fr] (foh bon-OMM)
> Seemingly friendly and generous, but in fact not.
faux frais [Fr]
> Incidentals, details.

faux ménage [Fr]
>An ill-matched married couple.

faux-naïf [Fr] (foh nah-EEF)
>Pretending to be sincere and honest.

faux pas [Fr] (foh pah)
>An indiscretion; a mistake; a social slip one regrets.

fecit [Lat] (FEH-kit)
>(He/she) made it. Seen on older paintings, sculpture, medals, coins, etc.

fee sehatak [Arab]
>Cheers!

fellah [Arab]
>In Arabic countries, a peasant.

femme de chambre [Fr] (fahm duh SHARM-bruh)
>Chambermaid.

femme fatale [Fr] (fahm fat-AHL)
>A seductress who brings woe and ruination to her lovers.

femme savante [Fr]
>Bluestocking.

fermatevi [It]
>Stop!

fermeture annuelle [Fr]
>The French summer holiday period in August when a good part of Paris shuts down and huge numbers of Parisians leave the city.

Ferry crossing

Amusing cross-fertilizations of English and French are not unknown on the cross-channel ferries. One fairly common loudspeaker announcement is, first in English: 'Ladies and gentlemen, the *buffet* is now open.' This is followed by the translation: '*Mesdames et messieurs, le* **snack bar** *est ouvert maintenant.*'

Ferragosto [It]
>The Italian bank holiday on August 15.

festina lente [Lat]
>More haste, less speed.

fête champêtre [Fr]
>An outdoor or country festival.

feu de joie [Fr] (fur duh ZHWAR)
>A sustained salute by rifle fire at public ceremonies.

feuilleton [Fr]
>A serialized novel; that part of a newspaper devoted to fiction or light reading.

fianchetto [It]
>In chess, the flank development of a bishop to control a key diagonal.

fiat Dei voluntas [Lat]
>God's will be done.

fiat lux [Lat]
>Let there be light.

Fidei Defensor [Lat] (fih-day-ee def-EN-sor)
>Defender of the Faith. The abbreviation ***Fid Def*** or ***FD***, can be seen on certain British coins.

fidus Achates [Lat]
>A faithful friend; an intimate companion.

filer à l'anglaise [Fr]
>Surreptitiously to slip away; to take 'French leave'.

fille de joie [Fr]
>A courtesan; prostitute.

fille du regiment [Fr]
>An army prostitute.

fils [Fr]
>Son. Used after the surname to distinguish the son from the father.

fin de siècle [Fr] (fa(n) duh SYEHK-(uhl))
>End of the century, specifically the end of the nineteenth century, with the suggestion of decadence and aestheticism.

71

fines herbes [Fr] (feen ZERB)
>   Mixed chopped herbs.

finis coronat opus [Lat]
>   The end crowns the work.

finita la commedia [It]
>   The comedy is over; the farce has ended.

fin sourire [Fr]
>   A knowing smile.

flambé [Fr]
>   Set alight. In cooking, to soak with brandy and
>   ignite just before serving.

flâneur [Fr] (fluh-NUR)
>   A loafer; idle man-about-town.

flecti, non frangi [Lat]
>   To be bent, not broken.

fleur-de-lis [Fr] (fluhr duh LEES)
>   Heraldic lily flower in the royal arms of France.

flic [Fr]
>   Cop; slang term for police.

floreat [Lat] (FLOH-rih-at)
>   May (it) flourish. The motto of Eton College:
>   **floreat Etona**.

folâtre [Fr]
>   Playful.

folie [Fr] (fol-ee)
>   Madness; delusions.

folie de grandeur [Fr] (fol-ee duh grah(n)-DUR)
>   Delusions of grandeur; illusions of greatness.

fondre en larmes [Fr]
>   To burst into tears.

force en frappe [Fr]
>   A strike force; now used to mean a nuclear
>   deterrent.

force majeure [Fr] (fors muh-ZHUR)
>   A superior, irresistible force; a compelling
>   circumstance that will release a party (e.g., an
>   insurance company) from fulfilling a contract.

foulard [Fr]
>   Headscarf or neckerchief.

fou qui se tait passe pour sage [Fr]
> A fool who holds his tongue passes for a wise man.

fraise [Fr]
> Strawberry. ***Fraises des bois*** = wild strawberries.

framboise [Fr]
> Raspberry.

frappé [Fr] (frah-pay)
> Chilled and iced; liqueur poured over crushed ice.

frapper [Fr]
> To strike; to knock. ***Entrez sans frapper*** = enter without knocking.

Frau [Ger] (frow)
> Married woman; equivalent to Mrs.

Fräulein [Ger] (FROY-leyn)
> Unmarried woman.

fraus est celare fraudem [Lat]
> It is fraud to conceal a fraud.

frequentasne hunc locum? [Lat]
> Do you come here often?

frère [Fr] (frair)
> Brother.

fresser [Yid]
> Glutton.

freundlich [Ger]
> Kind, friendly, genial.

fricassée [Fr]
> Stewed meat and vegetables served with a sauce.

fricatrice [Fr]
> Lesbian; female homosexual.

frijoles [Sp] (frih-HOLE-ays)
> Widely cultivated Mexican beans.

frisch auf! [Ger]
> Cheer up!

fritto misto [It] (free-toh mees-toh)
> Dish of mixed fried sea-food.

Fighting off *franglais*

French efforts to safeguard the purity of their language and to resist the nasty infection known as *franglais* is fairly well known. To their credit, the French care far more about their language than do users of English; we tend to welcome just about any new word from anywhere, cheerfully tolerate any novel usage and avert our gaze from serious word abuse.

The French, however, are proudly protective of their precise and elegant language. During the 1980s hundreds of foreign words were banned and official committees invented French words to replace them. *Animateur* replaced disc jockey; *navire-citerne* replaced tanker; *remue-meninges* replaced brainstorming; *ordinateur* replaced computer. The French also won the battle to name Concord **Concorde**, and insisted that in France a jet was *avion à réaction*.

Linguistic transgressors were hauled before the courts. TWA was fined for using English-language boarding passes at Charles de Gaulle Airport. Evian, the bottled water company, was fined for calling its new product '*le* fast drink *des Alpes*'. The Paris Opéra was sued for selling English-language programmes for the stage hit *Bubbling Brown Sugar*. A furniture maker was sued by Agulf (Association General for Users of the French Language) for using the term

Fröhliche Weihnachten! [Ger]
> Merry Christmas!

froideur [Fr] (frwar-dur)
> Cooling; a romantic relationship that's cooling off.

'showroom' instead of *salle d'exposition*.

But have the prohibitors succeeded? It appears not, for whatever officialdom may have decreed, French youth went its own freewheeling way, gobbling up western words from rock and pop albums and from the fashion, sporting, computer and business worlds. By the end of 1992 the venerable Académie française, the official arbiters of the language, bowed to partial defeat as it admitted 5,900 new words to the Gallic lexicon. Overnight, *le* **bestseller**, *le* **bookmaker**, *le* **bluejean**, *le* **clergyman**, *le* **cowboy**, *le* **dancing** and hundreds of other English words became officially French. Many others were accepted with the thinnest of veneers: bulldozer became *bouldozeur*; handshake became *shake-hand* and walkie-talkie became *talkie-walkie*. The surrender was, observed one academician, the only way to *solutionner un problème*.

However, the battle with *franglais* is not yet over. Under Gaullist culture minister Jacques Toubon the language-cleansing is being renewed with a draft bill promising new laws, fines and even jail sentences for using foreign words in newspapers, advertising and official documents. Perhaps Toubon should contemplate a French phrase that's long been a favourite *bon mot* in English: *c'est la vie*.

froides mains, chaud amour [Fr]
    Cold hands, warm heart.
fronti nulla fides [Lat]
    There is no trusting to appearances.

frou-frou [Fr] (froo-froo)
>   Originally the rustle of a woman's skirts; now
>   over-frilly, fussy ornamentation.

fruits de mer [Fr] (frwee duh MAIR)
>   Sea-food.

frustra laborat qui omnibus placere studet [Lat]
>   He labours in vain who attempts to please
>   everyone.

Fularno, Mengano y Zutano [Sp]
>   The Spanish equivalent of 'Tom, Dick and
>   Harry'. *Fularno* is used for 'So-and-so' when
>   referring to someone's name you can't
>   remember.

Funkstreife [Ger]
>   Police radio patrol.

furor scribendi [Lat]
>   A passion for writing.

Fürst der Schatten [Ger]
>   The Prince of Shades: death.

fustanella [It]
>   The stiff white cotton dress worn by Greek
>   soldiers during ceremonial occasions.

futsch [Ger]
>   Done for; had it: *der Wagen ist futsch* = the
>   car has had it.

G

gaieté de cœur [Fr]
>   Light-heartedness.

galette [Fr]
> The round, flat cake made to celebrate Twelfth Night on January 6. *Galette* is also slang for money.

gamine (fem); *gamin* (masc) [Fr]
> (gah-MEEN; gah-MAH(N))
> Having the impudence of a street urchin.

ganar [Sp] (gah-NAR)
> To make or win money.

gant de toilette [Fr]
> Wash cloth, the equivalent of the English flannel, although often a towelling glove.

garce [Fr]
> Slang for 'bitch'.

garçon [Fr] (GAR-sor(n))
> Waiter; boy.

gardez bien [Fr]
> Take good care.

gare [Fr]
> Railway station; platform. *Chef de gare* = station master; *Gare du Nord* = Northern Paris terminal.

gare! [Fr]
> Look out!

Gasthaus [Ger]
> Small inn or restaurant in Germany.

Gasthof [Ger]
> Hotel or inn in Germany.

gauche [Fr] (gohsh)
> Clumsy; socially inept.

gaudeamus igitur [Lat]
> (gow-day-ARM-us IG-ih-tur)
> Let us therefore rejoice! First line of the German students' drinking song.

gavroche [Fr]
> Street arab, from the gamin Gavroche in Hugo's *Les Misérables*.

gazpacho [Sp]
> Cold vegetable soup.

German

German is spoken by over 100 million people and is the official language of united Germany and Austria and the principal language of Switzerland. Of the two main varieties *Plattdeutsch* (Low German) and *Hochdeutsch* (High German), the Low variety has a strong affinity with English. If you visit Schleswig Holstein or anywhere along the north German coast, you will hear people saying they were born in 'neinteyn-hunder-fife-und-dirtig' (1935), talking about the 'veather' being 'colt' and asking you 'what ist duh klok?' You are, of course, in that part of Germany from which in the fifth century the Angles decided to move to what is now England, along with the Saxons and the Jutes. That is perhaps why, apart from the difficult grammar and the propensity for word-building (something as simple as a matchbox is called a *Streichholzschachtelchen*), the English have little difficulty with German pronunciation. Almost automatically we sense that

gefilte [Yid]
> Balls of seasoned minced fish cooked in broth.

gemütlich [Ger] (guh-MOOT-likh)
> Good-natured, kindly.

gens de bien [Fr]
> Respectable folk.

gens de couleur [Fr]
> Coloured folk

gesagt, getan [Ger]
> No sooner said than done.

Gesellschaft [Ger]
> Company; association; society.

au is pronounced as *ow* as in **Frau**
ei is pronounced as *eye* as in **Heine**
ie is pronounced as *ee* as in **diesel**
ee is pronounced as *ay* as in **Beethoven**
ch is pronounced as *kh* as in **Bach**
j is pronounced as *y* as in **Jaeger**
w is pronounced as *v* as in **Wagner**
z is pronounced as *ts* as in **Mozart**, and so on.

The Germans are not so protective as the French about their language (although the ***Deutscher Sprachverein***, the German Language Society, sniffs out transgressions and, to quote one example, insists that the wrestling hold called the hammerlock should be called ***Ellenbogengelenk-schlüssel***) and unsurprisingly it is becoming littered with westernisms: ***Pressekonferenzen**, no **komment**, off die **rekord**, der **Teenager**, das **Walkout**, ein **Steadyseller**, der **Cashflow*** are some random (and horrible) examples.

Gesellschafterin [Ger]
    Call-girl; hired female escort.
Gesetz ist mächtig, mächtiger ist die Not [Ger]
    The law is mighty but necessity is mightier (Goethe).
Gesundheit! [Ger] (guh-ZOONTH-hyt)
    Good health! Said to someone who sneezes; also used as a toast. ***Gesundheit is besser als Reichtum*** = health is better than riches.
geteilte Freude ist doppelte Freude [Ger]
    A joy shared is a joy doubled.
gettane le margherite ai porci [It]
    To throw pearls before swine.

Gewerkschaft [Ger]
> Trade union.

gigot [Fr] (zhee-goh)
> Leg of mutton.

gillie; ***ghillie*** [Gael]
> A helper or guide in the Scottish Highlands
> hunting regions.

giri [Jap]
> To observe one's moral duty in society.

gitano [Sp]
> Gypsy.

glacé [Fr] (glahs-say)
> Glazed; iced with sugar.

Glasgow German

When it was discovered that four Germans in the
dock of a Glasgow court could speak no
English, a man in the public gallery promptly
offered to interpret, saying that he had learned
the language as a prisoner of war.

The Sheriff then addressed the first German:
'What is your name?' (*Wie heißen Sie?*)

The interpreter translated: 'Vot iss your name,
hein?'. He was charged with contempt of court.

---

glasnost [Rus] (glas-nyast)
> Literally: publicity. Openness; receptive to
> criticism.

gloire [Fr] (glwahr)
> French patriotic sense of honour and glory.

gloria in excelsis Deo [Lat]
> Glory be to God on high. The prayer that
> follows the Kyrie of the Mass.

Glück auf! Glück zu! [Ger]
> Good luck! ***Glück auf den Weg*** = have a
> pleasant journey.

gnocchi [It] (nyok-kih)
> Dumplings, served with soup or sauce.

gombeen-man [Ir]
> Money-lender.

Gongchandang [Ch]
> Communist Party. **Gongchandangyuan** =
> Party member.

Gospodar [Rus]
> Gentleman.

Gospodin [Rus]
> Master. The equivalent to Mr or Sir.

Götterdämmerung [Ger]
> (gur-tuh-DEM-uh-rung)
> The twilight of the Gods; the end of the world.

Gott mit uns [Ger]
> God with us; motto of the Prussian kings.

Gott sei dank [Ger]
> God be thanked.

gouine [Fr]
> Crude term for a lesbian; female homosexual.

goûter [Fr]
> Literally: to taste. A kind of French afternoon
> tea or snack, indulged in at about 4 p.m.

gracias a Dios [Sp]
> Thanks to God.

gradatum vincimus [Lat]
> We conquer step by step.

graffito [It]
> Slogans, often indecent, painted or scratched
> on walls. The form most used is the plural,
> **graffiti**.

grande amoureuse [Fr] (grahnd am-uh-rurz)
> A woman who gives her life to love affairs.

grande dame [Fr] (grahnd dahm)
> Great lady; aristocratic.

grande école [Fr] (grahnd ay-kol)
> Colleges of higher education of which the *École
> Polytechnique* is one of the best known.

grande passion [Fr]
>   A passionate and serious love affair.

grande vedette [Fr]
>   A famous film or stage star.

Grand Guignol [Fr] (grah(n) GEE-nyol)
>   A short, macabre play intended to horrify.

grand mal [Fr] (grah(n) mal)
>   Violent form of epilepsy.

grand siècle [Fr]
>   The seventeenth century; the age of Louis XIV.

gran turismo [It]
>   High-performance touring car.

Is it all Greek to you?

Greek can be frustrating. The spoken language comes in a variety of local dialects, a classical version (***Katharevusa***) and the popular speech (***Demotic***) which is now the official state language.

Written Greek, at least when written in capital letters, looks accessible because much of the alphabet appears to resemble our own: A is **alpha**, B is **beta**, K is **kappa**, M is **mu** and so on. But it departs somewhere with letters which have no English equivalents: ψ or **psi** (pronounced **ps** as in **lapse**), X or **chi** (pronounced **ch** as in **loch**) and θ or **theta** (pronoucned **th** as in **thought**).

Here's a little quiz to tweek your Greek. Make six common words from the fragments below by inserting the names of Greek letters.
(Answers on page 84.)

1. m – – – llic   *4. ca – – – ze*
2. ca – – – p   *5. ma – – – nery*
3. – – – losophy   *6. res – – – rant*

grappa [It]
> Italian brandy made from grape pressings.

gratia gratiam parit [Lat]
> Kindness produces kindness.

gratin [Fr]
> Cooked with a crust of breadcrumbs and cheese.

gravad lax; ***gravlax*** [Swed]
> Dry-cured spiced salmon. ***Gravad strömming*** = dry-cured spiced herring.

graviora manent [Lat]
> The worst is yet to come.

grisette [Fr]
> Literally: grey dress fabric. A young working-class woman.

Groschenroman [Ger]
> The equivalent of English 'penny dreadful' novels, bodice rippers and wild west pulp novels.

gros mot [Fr]
> Colloquial for swear word.

guasto [It]
> A sign you see when something (telephone, lift, automatic dispensers etc.) is out of order.

guberniya [Rus]
> Administrative division of the former Soviet Union.

guerre à outrance [Fr]
> Total warfare; duel to the death.

Gum [Rus] (goom)
> State Universal Shop: the large Moscow department store.

gute Besserung [Ger]
> A wish for a speedy recovery.

Gymnasium [Ger]
> Grammar school. Pupils are 11–16 years but most stay for a further three years.

H

habeas corpus [Lat]
> Literally: You may have the body. A writ
> ordering a person to appear before the court
> to establish whether or not detention is lawful.

habitué [Fr]
> A regular customer.

habrit ha khadasha [Heb]
> The New Testament.

hacendado [Sp]
> A person owning property; proprietor of a
> **hacienda**.

hachimaki [Jap]
> The ubiquitous headbands worn by males to
> encourage concentration and effort.

hadj; **hajj** [Arab]
> The Muslim pilgrimage to Mecca.

hadji; **hajji** [Arab]
> A Muslim who has made the pilgrimage to
> Mecca.

haec olim meminisse juvabit [Lat]
> In time it will be pleasing to remember (these
> events).

haiku [Jap] (hy-koo)
> Japanese poem of just three lines and a total of

84

seventeen syllables arranged 5,7,5.

haka [Maori] (HAR-kuh)
> Maori war dance made familiar by the All
> Blacks rugby team before their games.

halal
> Meat from animals slaughtered according to
> Muslim law.

halászlé [Hung]
> Thick, paprika-flavoured fish soup.

Halbstarker [Ger]
> A teenage hooligan; a delinquent.

hapax legomenon [Gk]
> A word or saying unique in any written
> language; used only once.

hara-kiri [Jap]
> Literally: guts slit. Samurai suicide by
> disembowelling.

hare Krishna [Sanskrit]
> Hail to Krishna!

hashi [Jap]
> Chopsticks.

hasta la muerte todo es vida [Sp]
> Until death, all is life; while there's life there's
> hope.

hasta la vista [Sp]
> Goodbye.

haud fiet, et clavo fixum est [Lat]
> Nothing doing, and that's final!

Haus und Hof [Ger]
> House and home.

Hausfrau [Ger] (hows frow)
> German housewife – not generally
> complimentary.

haute bourgeoisie [Fr] (oht boor-zhwah-zee)
> The upper-middle or professional class.

haute couture [Fr] (oht kuh-TYOOR)
> High fashion dress design.

haute cuisine [Fr] (oht kwih-ZEEN)
> Top class cooking.

haute école [Fr]
>   Classical horse-riding.

heb' dich weg von mir, Satan [Ger]
>   Get thee behind me, Satan.

Heimat [Ger]
>   Home; one's birth-place.

Heimweh [Ger]
>   Home-sickness.

hendiadys [Lat via Gk]
>   A figure of speech in which two nouns are
>   linked by a conjunction for effect: **fear and
>   loathing, gloom and despondency**, etc.,
>   instead of **fearful loathing, gloomy
>   despondency**.

Herrenvolk [Ger]
>   Master race: Nazi term for the German people.

Herzchen [Ger]
>   Darling!

heute mir, morgen dir [Ger]
>   My turn today, yours tomorrow.

hic et ubique [Lat]
>   Here and everywhere.

hic jacet [Lat] (heek YAK-et)
>   Here lies (followed by name of deceased).

Himmel [Ger]
>   Heavens!

hinc illae lacrymae [Lat]
>   Literally: hence those tears. That's the cause.

hin ist hin [Ger]
>   Gone is gone; forget it.

Hinz und Kunz [Ger]
>   The equivalent of 'Tom, Dick and Harry';
>   sometimes ***Krethi*** und ***Plethi***.

hoch soll er leben [Ger]
>   Long may he live.

hoi polloi [Gk] (hoy-puh-LOY)
>   The masses; the common multitude.
>   Pedantically correct without 'the', but usage
>   now accepts ***the hoi polloi***.

¡hola! [Sp]
> Greeting to intimates and friends, roughly equivalent to 'hullo'.

homard [Fr] (om-mahr)
> Lobster.

homme d'affaires [Fr] (om dah-FAYR)
> A businessman.

homme de lettres [Fr] (om duh letruh)
> Man of letters.

homme du monde [Fr] (om doo MOR(N)D)
> A man of the world.

homo trium literatum [Lat]
> A thief. The phrase translates as 'three letter man' meaning ***fur***, Latin for thief.

honi soit qui mal y pense [Fr]
> Shame on him who thinks ill of it. Motto of the Order of the Garter.

hora fugit [Lat]
> The hour flies.

horresco referens [Lat]
> I shudder to tell.

horribile dictu [Lat] (hoh-REEB-ih-lay dik-too)
> Horrible to tell. The opposite is ***mirabile dictu*** = wonderful to tell.

hors concours [Fr] (or koh(n)-kor)
> Superior, therefore not in competition; not competing for any prize.

hors de combat [Fr] (or duh koh(n)-bah)
> Out of the fight; disabled.

hors d'œuvre [Fr] (or DURV-ruh)
> Appetizer before main course.

hôtel des postes [Fr]
> General post office.

hôtel de ville [Fr]
> Town hall.

hoteru [Jap]
> Hotel.

huîtres [Fr] (WEET-ruh)
> Oysters.

Hungarian

One of the first things you notice about Hungarian is the density of the diacriticals, including loads of umlauts and acres of acute accents – even double acutes. **Thank you** is rendered as *köszönöm szépen*; **spa** is *gyógyfürdöhely*. The chief reason for all those marks is that every vowel forms a syllable and all vowels are pronounced separately, even where several follow each other. Until you master the system you might as well be talking to a Tibetan. Forms of address are important in Hungary, too. There are three words for **you**: *te*, which is used when addressing family and children; the everyday *maga*, and the formal or polite *ön*. Confusing, yes; but not as confusing as having to go to the *Stomatológiai Intézet* for a dental emergency.

huzur [Arab]
> Your presence; polite form of address, as in 'Your Honour'.

hwyl [Welsh] (HOO-il)
> Religious or emotional fervour, as experienced with preaching, poetry reading, sporting events, etc.

I

ibidem*; *ibid [Lat] (IB-id-em)
> In the same place; used when referring to a
> quote previously cited.

Ich danke Ihnen [Ger]
> I thank you.

Ich dien [Ger] (ik-DEEN)
> I serve. Motto of the Prince of Wales.

Ich kann nicht anders [Ger]
> I can do no other. From a speech by Martin
> Luther; now used in the sense of standing by
> one's principles in the face of hostility.

Ich liebe dich [Ger] (eek leeb-uh deek)
> I love you.

Ici on parle français [Fr]
> French spoken here.

idée fixe [Fr] (eed-ay feeks)
> A fixed idea; obsession.

idem*; *id [Lat] (id-dem)
> The same. To avoid repetition used in footnotes
> to refer to an author already named.

Iesus Nazarenus Rex Iudaeorum [Lat]
> Jesus of Nazareth, King of the Jews. The initials
> ***INRI*** are often seen on paintings of the
> Crucifixion.

i frutti proibiti sono i piu dolci [It]
> Forbidden fruits are sweetest.

ignis fatuus [Lat]
> Will-o'-the-wisp, a phosphorescence seen in
> swamps and marshes. Used now to mean a
> delusion or a foolish idea.

Igiriss [Jap]
    Great Britain.
ikebana [Jap]
    The art of Japanese flower arranging.

Ill in France

The French have long been recognized as champion hypochondriacs. Before the big summer break newspapers run special supplements not on where to visit but on how to deal with holiday diseases and *le mal des transports* – travel sickness in all its rich variety: *sensation de vertige* (giddiness), *état nauséeux* (waves of nausea), *sueurs abondants* (profuse sweating), *accélération de rythme cardiaque* (erratic heartbeat) and *frissons* (shivering), not to mention *troubles digestifs avec vomissements* (stomach-ache with vomiting).

It is said that France is not a good country to get sick in. This is not to suggest that French medical care is in any way wanting; on the contrary, it is administered with morbid enthusiasm. The slightest sign of *constipe* – or, for that matter almost any malady – *alors!* – you'll have a box of *suppositoires* slapped into your hand. And don't, whatever you do, *avoir une crise de foie*, which is to have a liver crisis or, less dramatically, *l'indigestion*. The French live and die by their livers and regard good health as a temporary aberration to normal living. So if you wish to avoid what may well be *le remède est pire que le mal* (the cure is worse than the illness), consider the alternative: *mieux vaut prévenir que guérir* (prevention is better than cure).

Ik hou van je [Dut] (eek how van yuh)
>   I love you.

il faut cultiver son jardin [Fr]
>   We must cultivate our own garden – Voltaire.
>   We should attend to our own affairs.

il faut souffrir pour être belle [Fr]
>   We (women) must suffer to be beautiful.

illud Latine dici non potest [Lat]
>   You can't say that in Latin.

ils n'ont rien appris ni rien oublie [Fr]
>   They have learned nothing and forgotten
>   nothing. Said of the Court of Louis XVIII.

immer schlimmer [Ger]
>   From bad to worse.

immobiliste [Fr]
>   Someone who opposes change and progress.

imperméable [Fr]
>   Raincoat.

imposta sul valore aggiunto [It]
>   Known as ***IVA*** – the equivalent of Value Added
>   Tax (VAT).

in absentia [Lat]
>   In the absence (of the party concerned).

in alio loco [Lat]
>   In another place.

inamorato [It]
>   Lover. The feminine is ***inamorata***.

in bona partem [Lat]
>   (To be judged) favourably or sympathetically.

in camera [Lat]
>   Conducted in private, rather than in an open
>   court.

inconnu [Fr]
>   Unknown; someone whose identity is not
>   known.

Index Librorum Prohibitorum [Lat]
>   For four centuries (1564–1966) the list of
>   books prohibited or censored by the Roman
>   Catholic Church.

Indian

Of the Indian sub-continent's 950 million people, India's population of around 720 million share some 800 local languages, almost all of them mutually unintelligible. Obviously a lingua franca is vital for national communication and although English is not the official language (Hindi has been since 1965) a version of it – Indian English – is spoken by some 40 million and remains the language of culture, education and aspiration. English has absorbed many Indian words – **gymkhana**, **bungalow**, **copra**, **chintz**, **polo** and **pyjama** are just a few – and some millions of Britons who eat in Indian restaurants can claim familiarity with the names of a wide range of foods from the sub-continent.

in extenso [Lat]
> At full length; entire.

in extremis [Lat]
> At the point of death.

in flagrante delicto [Lat]
> In the very act.

infra dignitatem; *infra dig* [Lat]
> Beneath one's dignity.

in hoc signo vinces [Lat]
> By this sign thou shall conquer.

in loco parentis [Lat]
> In the place of a parent; with the responsibilities and authority of parents.

in nomine Patris et Filii et Spiritus Sancti [Lat]
> In the name of the Father, and of the Son, and of the Holy Spirit.

in perpetuum [Lat]
> For ever.

in puris naturalibus [Lat]
>   (in pyoo-ris nat-you-RAHL-ih-bus)
>   Starkers; naked.

in re [Lat]
>   In the matter of; concerning.

in saecula saeculorum [Lat]
>   For ever and ever; always.

insalutato hospite [Lat]
>   Leaving without saying farewell to your host.

in situ [Lat] (in SIT-yoo)
>   In its original place; undisturbed.

inter alia [Lat]
>   Among other things.

interregnum [Lat]
>   The period between reigns or rulers when the
>   state is governed by a temporary authority.

in toto [Lat]
>   Completely; entirely.

intoxicado [Sp]
>   *Está intoxicado* means 'He is poisoned', not 'He
>   is drunk'.

intoxication [Fr]
>   Poisoning. ***Intoxication alimentaire*** = food
>   poisoning. A notorious ***Faux Ami*** (*see article
>   on False Friends Page 00*).

intra vires [Lat] (in-truh VEE-rays)
>   Within the power and authority of a person or
>   institution.

in utero [Lat]
>   In the womb.

in vino veritas [Lat]
>   In wine there is truth; a drunk always speaks
>   the truth.

in vitro [Lat] (in VEET-roh)
>   In an artificial environment; in the laboratory.

in vivo [Lat]
>   In the living organism; in the body.

ipso facto [Lat]
>   By that very fact.

is iyian! [Gk]
>Cheers!

Italia para nacer, Francia para vivir, España para morir [Sp]
>Italy to be born in, France to live in, Spain to die in.

Italian

Most of us know enough about Italian to be aware that **c** before **e** or **i** is pronounced **ch** as in **church** and *ciao*; that **ch** is pronounced **k** as in *Chianti*; that the **g** of **gli** is silent as in *intaglio*; and that **z** and **zz** are pronounced **ts** as in *scherzo* and *intermezzo*. We know this because of the large number of Italian words that have been absorbed into English – especially in the fields of music, opera, food and drink – and because we continue to pronounce them the way the Italians do.

The Italians at home, however, find the going more complicated. Regional accents and dialects remain deep-rooted and millions of Italians have great difficulty communicating with their fellow citizens. This is where the verbal gesture fills the gap, making the language one of the most expressive at football matches and in traffic arguments: *Bastardo! Stronzo! Maladetto fottuto!*

Ivrit [Heb]
>Hebrew.

izvestia; izvestiya [Rus]
>Information; news. The title of one of the CIS's national newspapers.

J

j'accuse [Fr]

Emile Zola's famous public letter in *l'Aurore* to the government of France in 1898, for which he risked all to tell all and which was headlined *J'Accuse . . . !* has lent its name to any published accusation of injustice or intolerance.

jacta est alea [Lat]

The die is cast; there is no turning back. Said to have been spoken by Caesar when crossing the Rubicon.

j'adoube [Fr]

Literally: I adjust. To be said during a chess game before touching a piece to adjust it.

jai alai [Sp] (hy-uh-ly)

Ball game played with small baskets attached to a hand.

jalousie [Fr] (ZHAH-luh-zee)

Slatted window shutters.

jamais de ma vie [Fr]

Never in my life; emphatically never.

jamal [Arab]

Camel.

jambon [Fr]

Ham.

jardin des plantes [Fr]

Botanical garden.

jawohl [Ger] (yah-wohl)

Yes, certainly.

Japlish

Someone has estimated that since the end of the World War II the Japanese have engorged some 20,000 English words into their langauge – or approximately 10% of its lexicon. But when you look a little closer at this phenomenal appetite for words from the West you discover that in the process of digestion the English words have undergone a peculiar transformation. It has resulted in words that half-way resemble their English originals, and half-way sound like strangulated approximations of them. This new add-on to the Japanese language is called *Japlish*. Here are some examples:

erebeta	elevator	*bata*	butter
bifeteki	steak	*beisuboru*	baseball
Koka-	Coca-	*garafu*	golf
Kora	Cola	*huruts*	fruit
remon	lemon	*bijinesuman*	businessman
omuret	omelette		

Jehad; Jihad [Arab]
>A crusade inspired by strongly-held beliefs; specifically a Muslim holy war against unbelievers and enemies of Islam.

jellaba (*see also* **djellabah**) [Arab]
>The loose hooded cloak worn by Arab males.

je me'en fous [Fr]
>I don't care (vulgar).

je ne sais quoi [Fr]
>I don't know what . . . ; something indefinable; an indiscribable feeling.

je ne regrette rien [Fr]
>I regret nothing.

jenever [Dut]
>Dutch gin.

Some words, like **no-pan**, look and sound convincingly Japanese until you are told that it means bottomless waitress.

There exists, however, a world outside *Japlish*, where there is the increasing tendency amongst Japanese to use English words and phrases in contexts that are utterly meaningless. Try these:

- **Too old to die, too young to happy** – slogan on a cream soda.
- **Green piles** – brand of lawn fertilizer.
- **Pocket Wetty** – premoistened towelettes.
- **Fingernail Remover** – fingernail cleaner.
- **Hand-Maid Queer-Aid** – brand of chocolate bar.
- **Poccari Sweat** and **Homo Milk** – popular soft drinks.
- **Nazal** – *for stuffed nose and snot* – on nasal spray pack.

je t'aime [Fr] (jeh temm)
    I love you.
jeu de mots [Fr] (zhur duh moh)
    A play on words; for example, a pun.
jeu d'esprit [Fr] (zhur duh-spree)
    A light-hearted witticism or display of cleverness.
jeune fille [Fr] (zhurn fee-yuh)
    Young girl.
jiàngyóu [Ch]
    Soy sauce.
joie de vivre [Fr] (zhwah duh veev-ruh)
    Joy of life.

jolie-laide [Fr]
>See ***belle laide***.

jour de fête [Fr] (joor duh fayt)
>A feast day.

Judenhetze [Ger]
>Anti-Semitism.

ju-jitsu; ***jiu-jitsu*** [Jap]
>Japanese style of wrestling, using the opponent's strength to unbalance and throw him or her. ***judo*** is a refinement of ***ju-jitsu***.

julienne [Fr]
>Shredded vegetables, often made into soup by adding to meat broth.

junta [Sp] (DJYOON-tuh; HOON-tuh in the US)
>An unelected group, usually military officers, holding power.

jure divino [Lat]
>By divine right.

juste milieu [Fr] (joost mee-lyur)
>The happy medium; the golden mean; a middle course.

justification du tirage [Fr]
>Proof of the number of copies printed of limited edition books and prints.

j'y suis, j'y reste [Fr] (zhee-swee, zhee rest)
>Here I am, here I stay.

K

kabuki [Jap]
>Popular drama in Japan.

kafenio [Gk]
> Coffee-house where Greek coffee is served.

Kaffeeklatsch [Ger] (KAF-ay-klatsh)
> The gossip of a group (usually women) having coffee. Often mistakenly used to mean a 'coffee morning'.

kakemono [Jap]
> Japanese hanging scroll picture on rollers.

kalamarakia [Gk]
> Fried squid.

Kamerad [Ger]
> Comrade! Its use dates from World War I and was the cry of surrendering German soldiers.

Kampf der Anschauen [Ger]
> A conflict of opinions.

Kamooneesteechyeskaya partee-ya [Rus]
> Communist Party.

kan pei! [Ch]
> Bottoms up!; cheers!

Kapellmeister [Ger] (kah-PEL-meye-stuh)
> Orchestral or choir conductor.

kaput; kaputt [Ger]
> Done for; finished; had it.

karma [Sans]
> In Buddhism and Hinduism, the principle that a person's actions in the present life are responsible for that person's lot in a future reincarnation.

kashrut; kasher [Heb]
> Kosher.

Katzenjammer [Ger]
> Literally: the racket of mating cats. A monumental hangover.

Kaufhaus [Ger]
> Large department store.

kávé [Hung]
> Coffee.

Kazak [Rus]
> Cossack.

Keiner kann über sich sehn [Ger]
> No man can see beyond himself. By this
> Schopenhauer meant that nobody can
> appreciate the virtues of others without having
> some measure of those virtues within
> themselves.

Kellner [Ger]
> Waiter; inn porter.

kermesse [Fr]
> A village fair or carnival. The Dutch version is
> ***kermis***.

khabar*; *khubber [Hindi]
> Information; a news report.

khidmatgar [Hindi]
> Waiter or table servant.

Khmer [Mon-Khmer]
> Official language of Kampuchea, formerly
> Cambodia, and spoken by about five million
> people.

khushi*; *khosh [Hindi; Pers]
> Happiness; pleasure; comfort; to take one's
> pleasure. Via the Raj the English word **cushy**
> derives from it.

kibbutz [Heb]
> Israeli collective farm or communal industrial
> settlement. Plural: ***kibbutzim***. ***Kibbutznik*** =
> member of a ***kibbutz***.

kibitzer [Yid]
> Someone who interferes with unwanted advice.
> ***Kibitz*** is the verb = to interfere.

kiblah [Arab]
> The direction in which Muslims pray.

kiquette, la*; *quequette, la [Fr]
> Vulgar slang for penis.

Kinder, Kirche, Küche [Ger]
> Children, church, cooking – a woman's lot in
> life.

Kladderadatsch [Ger]
> A muddle; a mess.

Klappe [Ger]
> Mouth. *Halt die Klappe!* = shut up.

kleiner Mensch [Ger]
> Literally: small man. Narrow minded.

klutz [Yid]
> Someone clumsy and stupid. Often used in self-deprecation: 'What a klutz I am!'

knäckebröd [Swed]
> Crispbread.

Knesset [Heb]
> The Israeli parliament.

Köchel [Ger]
> Usually abbreviated to *K,* the letter preceding the catalogue number of Mozart's compositions; thus K525 is his *Eine Kleine Nachtmusik.* From Ludwig von Köchel (1800–1877) who first classified the musician's works.

kotzen [Ger]
> Colloquial for vomiting; *es ist zum Kotzen* = it's enough to make you sick!

krasi [Gk]
> Wine. *Krasi aspro* = white wine; *krasi kokino* = red wine.

Krasna-ya armee-ya [Rus]
> Red Army.

Kraut [Ger]
> Uncomplimentary word for a German, from Sauerkraut.

Kriminalroman; *Krimi* [Ger]
> Thriller novel.

Kripo [Ger]
> Colloquial shortening of *Kriminalpolizei,* the detective branch of the German police.

kukri [Hindi]
> Curved knife used by the Gurkhas.

kümmel [Ger]
> Liqueur flavoured with caraway.

kung fu [Ch]
> Chinese martial art derived from **karate** and **judo**.

Kunst ist die rechte Hand der Natur [Ger]
> Art is the right hand of Nature (Schiller).

kwela [Xhosa, Zulu] (kway-luh)
> Popular black music in South Africa, often featuring a penny whistle.

kvass [Rus]
> Russian beer made from grain and stale bread.

kyuji [Jap]
> Waiter.

L

la belle dame sans merci [Fr]
> Literally: the beautiful woman without mercy.

labore et honore [Lat]
> By labour and honour.

la critique est aisée et l'art est difficile [Fr]
> Criticism is easy and art is difficult.

lacrymae rerum [Lat]
> The tears of things; the sadness of life.

ladna [Rus]
> Okay.

Leavings from the Lahore Hotel

Egg amlate, egg boil, corn flax, french toss, fry toss, butter toss, jam toss, fruit custed, cack custed, milk shik. Club sand whiches are Chicken Katlas. Snakes.

> – *from the menu of the Lahore Hotel, Khanewal, Pakistan*

---

la donna è mobile [It]

Woman is a fickle thing. The title of a song from Verdi's *Rigoletto*.

laissez-aller; ***laisser-aller*** [Fr] (les-ay ah-lay)

Lack of constraint; letting things go; total freedom.

laissez-faire; ***laisser-faire*** [Fr] (les-ay fair)

The policy of non-intervention, of not interfering, especially by a government.

lait [Fr] (lay)

Milk. ***Au lait*** = with milk.

La Manche [Fr] (lah mah(n)sh)

The English Channel.

lambris d'appui [Fr]

Wall panelling that rises to about a metre from the floor. ***Lambris de hauteur*** = floor to ceiling wall panelling.

Land [Ger]

Country. ***Länder*** = German states. ***Landtag*** = legislature of a German state.

Landstraßenschreck [Ger]

Colloquial: road hog; rotten driver.

Langlauf [Ger]

Cross-country or long-distance skiing.

langouste [Fr]

Small spiny rock lobster.

langoustine [Fr]

Small crayfish; large prawns.

lapin [Fr]

Rabbit.

la propriété c'est le vol [Fr]

Property is theft – Proudhon.

lapsus calami [Lat] (lap-sus KAL-uh-mee)

A slip of the pen.

lapsus linguae [Lat] (lap-sus LING-way)

Slip of the tongue.

lapsus memoriae [Lat] (lap-sis memo-OR-ee-ay)

Slip of the memory.

Latin

Latin is a dead tongue, as dead as dead can be,
First it killed the Romans; now it's killing me.
All are dead who wrote it,
All are dead who spoke it,
All are dead who learned it.
Lucky dead – they've earned it.

For a dead language, though, Latin is
surprisingly persistent: about half the English
words we use in everyday speech, like **video**,
propaganda and **referendum** are derived from
it, or still survive intact – like *post mortem*, *per
annum* and *ad infinitum*. The language arrived
in Britain with the Romans, fought it out with
the Vikings and the Normans, and had a great
revival in the Renaissance with the rediscovery
of classical texts. That, however, was its
undoing. It was taken up by the church and the
scholars and refined into an esoteric code
understood only by the privileged few.

larmes dans la voix [Fr]
> Literally: tears in the voice. The quaver in the
> voice that precedes tears.

l'art pour l'art [Fr] (lah poor lah)
> Art for art's sake, free of practical, social and
> moral restrictions.

lasciate ogni speranza voi ch'entrate [It]
> All hope abandon, ye who enter here:
> inscription over the gates of Hell from Dante's
> *Inferno*.

lass das Vergang'ne vergangen sein [Ger]
> Let bygones be bygones: from Goethe's *Faust*.

latet anguis in herba [Lat]
> There's a snake in the grass; something is
> concealed.

Latin's decline continues. In the thirty years
to 1992, the Queen's *annus horribilis*, the
number of students taking O-Level Latin shrank
from 60,000 to under 14,000 – less than 2% of
children sitting GCSEs. Another ominous move
was the abandonment of Latin – for centuries
used by doctors and chemists to preserve their
secrets – by the *British Medical Journal*. And
then Vatican II decreed the vernacular Mass.

And yet, if you've grazed through some of the
hundreds of Latin entries in this book, you'll
agree that it possesses the economical and
elegant knack of turning a thought into an
indelibly memorable phrase. Why, even Waltzing
Matilda has its Latin rendering:

> *Veni Matilda, veni Matilda,*
> *Veni saltemus Matilda veni,*
> *Et cantabat homo dum aestuaret cortina:*
> *Veni saltemus Matilda veni.*

---

lato sensu [Lat]
>   In the broad sense.

latte [It]
>   Milk. *Latte condensato* = condensed milk;
>   *latte detergente* = cleansing milk; *latte
>   scremato* = skimmed milk.

lauda la moglie e tiente donzello [It]
>   Praise a wife and married life but stay single.

lavabo [Lat] (lah-VAR-boh)
>   Literally: I shall wash. The ritual washing of
>   hands after offertory at Mass. In Italian and
>   French, a washbasin or bathroom sink. In
>   French a fairly common euphemism for the
>   lavatory.

Lebensabend [Ger]
>   The twilight of life.

leben Sie wohl! [Ger]
>   Goodbye!

Lebensmut [Ger]
>   Zest for life.

Lebensraum [Ger]
>   Literally: living space. Territory claimed by a
>   country for its expanding population. Especially
>   applicable to Nazi Germany's annexation of
>   border territory.

leben und leben lassen [Ger]
>   Live and let live.

Leberwurst [Ger]
>   Liver sausage.

lechyd da! [Welsh]
>   Good health!

le coût en ôte le goût [Fr]
>   The cost spoils the taste.

leche [Sp]
>   Milk, but **mala leche** is 'bad blood' and also
>   vulgarly colloquial for semen.

le fin mot [Fr]
>   The key point; the gist.

Légion d'honneur [Fr] (lay-zhor(n) doh-NUR)
>   Legion of Honour, a civil or military order of
>   merit introduced by Napoleon in 1802.

leitmotiv; **leitmotif** [Ger]
>   Repeated theme, word, phrase, etc.

le meilleur vin a sa lie [Fr]
>   Even the finest wine has dregs.

le monde [Fr]
>   The world; mankind; society.

le mot de l'énigme [Fr]
>   The key to the mystery.

le mot juste [Fr] (luh moh-zhoost)
>   The exact word; the perfect word for the
>   purpose.

106

l'envoi [Fr]
>A postscript; a concluding verse or stanza.

le petit caporal [Fr]
>The little corporal: Napoleon.

le roi est mort; vive le roi [Fr]
>The king is dead; long live the king.

le Roi Soleil [Fr]
>Louis XIV: the Sun King.

les cinq lettres [Fr]
>Four-letter words.

lèse-majesté [Fr] (layz-MAH-zhest-ay)
>High treason; an offence against the sovereign
>power of a state. In a watered-down sense, an
>attack on arrogant or pompous authority.

les petites gens [Fr]
>Humble people.

l'état, c'est moi [Fr] (lay-tah, sah-mwar)
>I am the State. Attributed to Louis XIV.

le tout ensemble [Fr]
>Overall effect.

le vice anglais [Fr] (luh vees ah(n)-glay)
>Male homosexuality.

lex non scripta [Lat]
>Unwritten or common law.

lex talionis [Lat]
>Law of revenge; of retaliation.

liberté, égalité, fraternité [Fr]
>Liberty, equality, fraternity. Motto of France.

libro cerrado no saca letrado [Sp]
>An unopened book never made a scholar.

licenciado [Sp]
>Licenciate; a university graduate.

licencié [Fr]
>A university graduate, but *un licenciement*
>means to be given the sack.

Licht, Liebe, Leben [Ger]
>Light, love and life.

Liebchen [Ger]
>Darling! Beloved!

Liar's Latin

One of the oldest games to be played with Latin is to invent new meanings to sayings which look genuine but aren't. Here's a small collection to which you can add your own fabrications:

Sui generis: large serving of Chinese pork. *Hic jacet*: polyester sports coat. *De gustibus non est disputandem*: don't argue with the bus driver. *Reductio ad absurdum*: anorexia nervosa. *Et tu, Brute*: and two bottles of men's cologne, please. *Ex cathedra*: defrocked bishop. *Lapsus linguae*: lunch served on the Irish airline. *Summa cum laude*: God, it's hot! *Terra firma*: scared stiff. *ibid*: the noise made by a frog. *Ad hoc*: this dish needs wine.

Liebeserklärung [Ger]
> A declaration of love.

Liebe wintert nicht [Ger]
> Love knows no winter.

Lieb und Leid [Ger]
> Joy and sorrow.

lied; lieder [Ger] (LEED-uh)
> German song, usually a solo with piano. The plural is *lieder*.

limbus fatuorum [Lat]
> A fool's paradise.

lingua franca [It]
> A blend of Italian and other Mediterranean languages; nowadays any common language used by people with different mother tongues.

literae humaniores [Lat]
> Oxford faculty concerned with Greek and Latin; the Classics.

litera scripta manet [Lat]
> The written word remains; it is always wise to put it in writing.

littérateur [Fr] (lih-teh-ruh-TUR)
> A writer; man of letters.

livre de chevet [Fr]
> A favourite book; a companion book.

locum tenens [Lat]
> Someone who replaces a professional colleague during an absence, especially doctors and dentists.

locus classicus [Lat]
> The authoritative statement on a subject.

loden [Ger]
> Green-grey woollen material used to make traditional Bavarian peasant clothing; now fashionable for all kinds of clothing.

l'oeil du maître [Fr]
> The expert eye of the master.

logiciel [Fr]
> Computer software. It has been largely displaced by ***le software*** (*see article on Fighting off* franglais, page 74).

longueur [Fr] (lor(n)-GER)
> A long and tedious passage in a book, play, musical concert or speech.

lotteria [It]
> State lottery.

Lottoannahme [Ger]
> State lottery office.

louange perfide [Fr]
> Literally: treacherous praise. False praise intended to subvert and bring someone down.

lucri cause [Lat]
> For the sake of gain.

Lui è sbronzo [It]
>Vulgar colloquialism for 'he is very drunk'.

Lumpenproletariat [Ger]
>The disadvantaged, unambitious poor.

l'union fait la force [Fr]
>Unity makes strength.

L'uomo propone, Dio dispone [It]
>Man proposes, God disposes.

lupus in fabula [Lat]
>Literally: the wolf in the fable. The unexpected appearance of someone just as he or she is being talked about.

lusus naturae [Lat]
>A freak of nature; one of nature's jokes.

lux et veritas [Lat]
>A light in the darkness.

lux mundi [Lat]
>Light of the world.

lycée [Fr] (LEE-say)
>French secondary school.

M

maa as-salaamah [Arab]
>Goodbye.

ma biche [Fr]
>Literally: my doe. My darling.

macchabée [Fr]
>Corpse. Also colloquially ***un macab***.

machismo; macho [Sp]
>   Pride in masculinity,

Macht ist Recht [Ger]
>   Might is right.

Machtpolitik [Ger]
>   Power politics.

ma chère [Fr] (mar-shair)
>   My dear (address only to women).

machin [Fr]
>   Equivalent to English 'thingummy' or 'wotsit'.

Mädchen [Ger]
>   Girl; maiden.

madeleine [Fr]
>   Small sweet cake.

Mae hen wlad fy nhadau [Welsh]
>   The land of my fathers: Welsh national anthem.

magari [Gk]
>   If only it were so!

maggiore fretta, minore alto [It]
>   More haste, less speed.

magister ceremoniarum; MC [Lat]
>   Master of ceremonies.

magna cum laude [Lat] (mag-nah kum-LOW-dih)
>   With great distinction.

magna est veritas et praevalebit [Lat]
>   Truth is great and shall prevail.

Magnificat [Lat] (mag-NIF-ih-kat)
>   Hymn of the Virgin Mary: 'My soul doth
>   magnify the Lord'; any hymn of praise.

magnum opus [Lat]
>   Masterpiece; an artist's greatest work.

Magyarország [Hung]
>   Hungary. A Hungarian is a **Magyar férfi**
>   (man) or a **Magyar nö** (woman).

maharani [Hindi]
>   A maharajah's wife or widow.

maharishi [Hindi]
>   Hindu seer or wise man.

mahatma [Sans]

Exponent of Buddhism; a sage.

Mahayana [Sans]

A liberal branch of Buddhism.

maidan [Urdu]

In India and Pakistan a space for meetings or a sportsground.

maillot jaune [Fr]

The yellow jersey worn by the leader in the *Tour de France* cycle race.

mains froides, coeur chaud [Fr]

Cold hands, warm heart.

mairie; **maire** [Fr]

French town hall and mayor respectively.

maison de passe [Fr]

A disreputable hotel, most likely a brothel. Such an establishment is also called a **maison de société** and a **maison de tolérance**, the latter being licensed.

maison de santé [Fr]

Private hospital; nursing home.

maître d'hôtel [Fr]

Hotel head-waiter.

maître de ballet; **maîtresse de ballet** [Fr]

Person who trains and rehearses a ballet company.

maîtresse en titre [Fr]

A man's recognized mistress.

makimono [Jap]

Japanese scroll painting that unrolls horizontally.

maladresse [Fr]

Clumsiness; lack of tact.

mal à propos [Fr]

Literally: not to the purpose. Inappropriate. The word supplied Sheridan the inspiration for Mrs Malaprop for his play *The Rivals*, hence **malapropism**: the unintentional misuse of words with similar sounds.

mal d'amour [Fr]
>   Love-sick.

mal de mer [Fr] (mal duh mair)
>   Sea-sickness. Other **mals** include **mal au
>   cœur** = nausea; **mal au ventre** = stomach
>   ache; **mal de tête** = headache; **mal de dents** =
>   toothache.

mal du siècle [Fr]
>   World weariness; weariness of life.

male parta, male dilabuntur [Lat]
>   Easy come, easy go.

malgré tout [Fr] (mal-gray TOO)
>   In spite of everything.

malheur ne vient jamais seul [Fr]
>   Troubles never come singly.

mal mariée [Fr]
>   An unhappily married woman.

Mamma mia! [It]
>   My mother!

mammismo [It]
>   Maternal control and interference by a mother
>   that continues even when the family is fully
>   grown.

mañana [Sp]
>   Tomorrow. Sometime.

mancia [It]
>   **una mancia** = a tip or gratuity.

manqué [Fr]
>   Unfulfilled; failed; would-be: 'Like most of his
>   crowd he was just a writer **manqué**.'

manque de goût [Fr]
>   Lack of good taste.

man spricht Deutsch [Ger]
>   German spoken.

maquerelle [Fr]
>   The madam of a brothel.

maquillage [Fr]
>   Cosmetics; make-up.

marché [Fr]
>
> Market. *Un marché decouvert* = an open-air market; *Marché Commun* = (European) Common Market.

mare nostrum [Lat]
>
> The Mediterranean.

mariage de convenance [Fr]
>
> (mar-ih-arzh duh koh(n)-veh-nah(n)s)
> Marriage of convenience, usually with financial motive.

Marianne [Fr]
>
> Symbol of republican France and much prettier than John Bull or Uncle Sam.

marinare [It]
>
> To pickle; to marinate.

Mark Twain on the French language

'In Paris they simply stared when I spoke to them in French; I never did succeed in making those idiots understand their own language . . .'

---

marmite [Fr] (mah-MEET)
>
> Pot or saucepan.

marron glacé [Fr]
>
> Crystallized chestnut.

mashallah [Arab]
>
> God has willed it.

masjid; *musjid* [Arab]
>
> An Islamic mosque.

mas vale tarde que nunca [Sp]
>
> Better late than never.

materfamilias [Lat]
>
> The mother or female head of the family.

matryoshka [Rus]
>
> Traditional Russian decorative dolls.

matzo; *matza* [Heb]
>
> Crisp unleavened bread eaten at Passover.

mauvais coucheur [Fr] (moh-vay koo-shur)
Argumentative, cantankerous person.

mauvais foi [Fr] (moh-vay fwahr)
Bad faith.

mauvais goût [Fr] (moh-vay goo)
Bad taste.

mauvais moment [Fr]
An unpleasant and embarrasing moment.

mauvais sang [Fr]
Bad feeling; bad blood.

mauvais sujet [Fr] (moh-vay soo-zhay)
A 'black sheep'.

maxima cum laude [Lat]
With the highest praise and distinction.

maxima debetur puero reverentia [Lat]
The greatest reverence is due to a child
(Juvenal); a child should be protected from
vulgarity and indecency.

mea culpa [Lat]
The fault is mine; it's my fault.

médecine expectante [Fr]
Nature's cure; medical treatment left to Nature.

medice, cura te ipsum [Lat]
Physician, heal thyself.

meditatio fugae [Lat]
Contemplating flight from justice.

Megali Vretania [Gk]
Great Britain.

megillah [Yid]
An unnecessarily long and tiresome story or
letter. From the Hebrew ***Megillah***, the scroll
of the Book of Esther.

Mehr Licht! [Ger]
More light! Goethe's last words, 1832.

Mehrwertsteuer [Ger]
Value added tax.

mein Gott! [Ger]
My God!

Mein Kampf [Ger]
>*My Struggle*: Adolf Hitler's 1924 autobiography.

mélange [Fr] (mah-lah(n)zh)
>A mixture; a confusion.

mêlée [Fr] (meh-lay)
>A confused affray; an unruly scramble.

melioribus annis [Lat]
>In happier times.

membrum virile [Lat]
>Penis.

memento mori [Lat]
>A reminder of death; a symbolic reminder (e.g. a skull) of death.

ménage [Fr] (mah-nahzh)
>A household; housekeeping.

ménage à trois [Fr] (may-nahzh uh TRWAH)
>A domestic arrangement of husband and wife and a lover of one or both of them.

menefreghista [It]
>Like Rhett Butler, someone who doesn't give a damn.

mens rea [Lat] (mens ray-ah)
>With criminal intent; with the knowledge that an action is a criminal offence.

mens sana in corpore sano [Lat]
>A healthy mind in a healthy body.

menus plaisirs [Fr]
>For life's little pleaures; pocket money.

méprisable [Fr]
>Contemptible.

merci [Fr] (mair-see)
>Thank you.

merde [Fr] (maird)
>Excrement; shit. *Le merdier* = a mess.

meret qui laborat [Lat]
>He is deserving who is industrious.

mésalliance [Fr] (mah-ZAL-ih-ah(n)s)
>A marriage with a partner who is socially inferior.

meschugge; *meshugah* [Yid]
> Mad; silly; daft; crazy.

messaggero [It]
> Messenger. The title of one of Italy's big national newspapers.

métèque [Fr]
> An alien; a foreigner.

métis [Fr] (may-tee)
> Someone of mixed blood. In Canada of mixed American-Indian and French-Canadian blood; in the US know as an octoroon.

metteur au point [Fr]
> Someone who provides the solution to a problem.

meum et tuum [Lat] (May-um et too-um)
> Mine and thine: the principle of the rights of property.

mezé [Turk] (mez-eh)
> Greek and near-Eastern appetizers served with drinks.

miches [Fr]
> Vulgar slang in France for breasts.

Midi [Fr]
> The coastal plain contained by the Massif Central, Pyrenees and Alps in southern France.

midinette [Fr]
> Parisian shop assistant, usually in a dressmaker's or milliner's.

mierda [Sp]
> Spanish equivalent of *'merde'*.

mieux vaut tard que jamais [Fr]
> Better late than never.

mignon [Fr] (meen-yoh(n))
> Small and dainty.

mijnheer [Dut]
> Dutch equivalent to 'Sir'.

Milchmädchenrechnung [Ger]
> Literally: milkmaid's reckoning. A conclusion

or speculation based on faulty reasoning.

mille feuilles [Fr] (meel FUR-yih)
   Iced puff pastry cakes filled with jam and cream.

millefiori [It] (mee-leh-FYOR-ih)
   Ornamental glassware which features flower patterns.

mille verisimili non fanno un vero [It]
   A thousand probabilities make not a single truth.

Minglish,
or menus in mangled English

English travellers have for many years taken great delight in returning home with memories of distant cuisines expressed in a droll form of mangled English known as **Minglish**. Here are some four-star examples for which you must supply your own translations:

Ho-made pie	**Chicken smashed**
Utmost of chicken as	**pot**
Hungarian	**Boiled steam**
Birds inward parts	**Glassy sheep bones**
Pastry not special	**Thick intestine**
Bowel of origan	**Shrimbs lumps**
Lumps with blight	**Macaronis with ma**

and all washed down with

Big rottle beer   and   **Metallic water**

---

mirabile dictu [Lat] (mih-RARB-ih-lay DIK-too)
   Wonderful to relate.

mise-en-scène [Fr]
   The stage setting for a play.

Miserere [Lat] mih-zer-AIR-ay)
> Have mercy. ***Miserere mei, Deus*** = Have
> mercy on me, Lord: the 51st Psalm.

missa solemnis [Lat] (MIS-suh soh-LEM-nis)
> Roman Catholic High Mass.

Mist [Ger]
> Colloquially, 'manure' rather than 'shit'. Its
> English equivalent would be 'rubbish'.

mistral [Fr]
> The infamous wind that blows from the Massif
> Central across the south of France.

mit Gewalt [Ger]
> By force; by compulsion.

mit gleicher Münze zahlen [Ger]
> To repay tit for tat.

Mitteleuropa [Ger]
> Central Europe, especially the Balkans.

modus operandi [Lat]
> The way it works; method of operation.

modus vivendi [Lat]
> Agreement to differ; a compromise
> arrangement between two parties in dispute.

mœurs [Fr]
> Manners; customs.

moment de vérité [Fr]
> Moment of truth.

momzer [Yid]
> Literally: bastard. A contemptible person.

mon ami [Fr]
> My friend. Feminine form is ***mon amie***.

mon cher [Fr]
> My dear. Feminine form is ***ma chère***.

mon chéri [Fr]
> My darling. Feminine form is ***ma chérie***.

mon Dieu! [Fr] (mor(n) dyur)
> My God!

mont-de-piété [Fr]
> Licensed pawnshop, now known as ***Crédit
> Municipal***. The equivalent in Spain is ***monte***

de piedad, and in Italy, *monte di pietà*.

Mord mit Messer und Gabel [Ger]
> Colloquial: death from over-eating.

Morgenstunde hat Gold im Munde [Ger]
> Literally: The morning hour has gold in its mouth. As the English version has it: 'Early to bed, early to rise, makes a man healthy, wealthy and wise.'

morgue anglaise [Fr]
> English condescension.

morituri te salutant [Lat]
> We who are about to die salute you. This was the gladiatorial salute to the Roman emperors.

morta la bestia, morto il veneno [It]
> When the beast is dead he cannot bite.

mot juste
> See *le mot juste*.

motu proprio [Lat]
> Of one's free will.

moules [Fr]
> Mussels. **Moules marinière** = mussels served with a wine sauce.

mudéjar [Sp]
> Moorish-influenced architectural style in Spain.

muezzin [Arab]
> In Muslim countries, the crier who calls the faithful to prayer.

mucho en el suelo, poco en el cielo [Sp]
> Rich on earth, poor in the hereafter.

muito falar, pouco saber [Port]
> Many words, little knowledge.

multa cadunt inter calicem supremaque labra [Lat]
> There's many a slip 'twixt cup and lip.

multi sunt vocati, pauci sunt electi [Lat]
> Many are called; few are chosen.

multis terribilis, caveto multos [Lat]
> If many fear you, beware of many.

multum in parvo [Lat]
> Much in a small space.

Mumienschänder [Ger]
> 'Mummy decorator'. A 'toy boy'; a young gigolo.

muor giovane colui ch'al cielo è caro [It]
> Whom the gods love dies young.

Murkin

There are an estimated 250 million users of Murkin, or American English. Although most users of British English have little trouble understanding basic Murkin, deep Murkin is something else; ***Kohl arnjews? Skedada'eer!*** (Cold orange juice? Let's get out of here!) A Murkin dictionary is no doubt in preparation, but meanwhile here's some help:

Texan Murkin	***bar*** = borrow; ***dense*** = dentist; ***mere*** = mirror
Brooklyn Murkin	***toidy-toid an' toid*** = Thirty-third and Third
Mairlin Murkin (Maryland)	***Bollamuh*** = Baltimore; ***hoskul*** = high school; ***clays*** = clothes; ***par-me*** = pardon me

---

mutatis mutandis [Lat]
> The necessary or appropriate changes having been made.

Mütterchen [Ger]
> Grandma; old woman.

muu-muu [Hawaiian]
> Light, loose, and often colourful dress.

muzhik; ***moujik***, ***mujik*** [Rus]
>   Russian peasant.

Myetro [Rus]
>   Moscow underground railway system.

N

nach und nach [Ger]
>   Little by little.

Nacktkultur (*also **Freikörperkultur***) [Ger]
>   Naturism; the cult of nudism.

Nagy-Britannia [Hung]
>   Great Britain.

naïf [Fr] (nah-eef)
>   Artless; ingenuous.

naschen [Ger]
>   To eat sweets when one shouldn't. The Yiddish
>   term ***nosh*** = food derives from this.

nasi goreng [Dutch/Indonesian]
>   Spiced rice dish topped with egg.

natura abhorret a vacuo [Lat]
>   Nature abhors a vacuum.

natura il fece, e poi roppe la stampa [It]
>   Nature made him, then broke the mould.

n'avoir pas le sou [Fr]
>   To be without a sou; broke.

nazionale [It]
>   ***La Nazionale*** = Italy's national football team.
>   ***Un nazionale*** = an international player. For
>   more on ***il calcio*** – Italy's national game – see
>   ***scudetto***.

nebech; nebbish [Yid]
> A weak, ineffectual individual.

nec habeo, nec careo, nec curo [Lat]
> I have not, I want not, I care not.

ne choisit pas qui emprunte [Fr]
> He who borrows has no choice.

née [Fr] (nay)
> Literally: born. Her maiden name being . . .
> Follows a woman's married name and
> indicates her original surname: Lucinda Black,
> *née* White.

nemine dissentiente [Lat]
> Nobody dissents, nobody opposes.

nemo dat quod non habet [Lat]
> No one can give what he does not possess.

nemo me impune lacessit [Lat]
> No one injures me with impunity (Motto of
> Scotland).

nemo mortalium omnibus horis sapit [Lat]
> No one is wise at all times.

ne plus ultra [Lat]
> Literally: no more beyond. The pinnacle; the
> ultimate in perfection.

Neujahr [Ger]
> New Year.

Nicht alles, was glänzt ist Gold [Ger]
> All is not gold that glitters.

nihil ad rem [Lat]
> Irrelevant; not to the point.

Nihon [Japan]
> Japan. *Nihon-jin* = Japanese person.
> *Nihongo* = Japanese language.

nil bastardo carborundum [Liar's Latin]
> Don't let the bastards grind you down.

nil desperandum [Lat]
> Never despair.

nil mortalibus arduum est [Lat]
> Nothing is beyond the accomplishment of
> mortals.

nisi [Lat] (ny-sye)
>A decree that takes effect from a certain date unless cause is shown why it should not.

noblesse oblige [Fr] (noh-bless oh-BLEEZH)
>Originally the obligation of the nobility and aristocracy to act honourably; rank imposes obligations.

Noh; ***Nō*** [Jap]
>Elaborate stylized traditional Japanese drama.

noisette [Fr] (nwah-zet)
>Small, round boneless cut of lamb; hazelnut.

nolens volens [Lat]
>Whether willing or unwilling; having no alternative.

noli irritare leones [Lat]
>Don't annoy the lions.

noli me vocare, ego te vocabo [Lat]
>Don't call me, I'll call you.

nolle prosequi [Lat]
>Official abandonment of a legal action or a prosecution.

nom de guerre [Fr] (nom-duh-gair)
>An assumed name or pseudonym. The French equivalent of the anglicized ***nom de plume***.

non compos mentis [Lat]
>Of unsound mind.

non generant aquilae columbas [Lat]
>Eagles do not bear doves.

non mi ricordo [It]
>I don't remember.

non possumus [Lat] (non pos-SOOM-us)
>Literally: we cannot. In law, inability to act in a matter.

non ragioniamo di loro, ma guarda e passa [It]
>From Dante: 'Speak not of them, but look and pass them by'.

non sapere l'abbicci [It]
>Literally: not to know the alphabet. To be abysmally ignorant.

- *non so* [It]
>   I don't know – a phrase that infiltrates all
>   everyday Italian speech as a 'sentence filler',
>   equivalent to the English 'um . . . y'know'.

Norwegian

Norway fascinates philologists because it has two
written languages. After the dissolution of its
union with Denmark in 1814 the country found
itself saddled with Danish, which didn't fit at
all with national aspirations. Throughout the
nineteenth century Norway had to reinvent its
own language, starting out with a mixture of
Danish and native spoken Norwegian
(**Riksmål**) and finishing up, at the end of the
century, with **Bokmál**, or book language, and
Nynorsk, or New Norwegian. Both are now
taught in bilingual Norway where the
inhabitants customarily blend the two according
to their geographic background and social
status. Learning two languages may have honed
their linguistic skills; a large number of
Norwegians speak excellent English.

---

nos dah [Welsh]
>   Good-night.

nostalgie de la boue [Fr]
>   The perverse yearning of civilized people for
>   sordid and degrading experiences.

nota bene; *NB* [Lat]
>   Note well; take notice.

Not bricht Eisen [Ger]
>   Necessity breaks iron; equivalent to 'necessity
>   is the mother of invention'.

nous [Gk]
> Reason. Colloquially, in English, it means common sense or intelligence.

nous verrons ce que nous verrons [Fr]
> We shall see what we shall see.

nouveau riche [Fr] (noo-voh reesh)
> Someone who has recently become wealthy but is regarded as socially inferior.

novus homo [Lat]
> A new man; an ***arriviste***; an upstart.

nuda veritas [Lat]
> Naked truth.

nudis verbis [Lat]
> In plain words.

nudnik [Yid]
> A bore.

nul bien sans peine [Fr]
> There's no gain without pain.

nulla mensa sine impensa [Lat]
> There's no free lunch.

nulla nulla [Abor]
> Club used as a weapon by Australian aborigines.

nulla nuova, buona nuova [It]
> No news is good news.

nulli desperandum, quamdiu spirat [Lat]
> While there's life, there's hope.

nulli secundus [Lat]
> Second to none.

nullo modo [Lat]
> No way!

nunc aut nunquam [Lat]
> Now or never.

nunc dimittis [Lat]
> From the first line of the Latin version of Simeon's Canticle: 'Lord, now lettest thou thy servant depart in peace.'

nunc est bibendum [Lat]
> Now is the time for drinking.

nunquam dormio [Lat]
> I never sleep; I am always on my guard.

nyet [Rus]
> No.

O

obi [Jap]
> The wide sash with a bow at the back, worn as part of their national costume by Japanese women.

obiter dictum [Lat] (OB-ih-ter DIK-tum)
> An incidental comment or observation. In law, a relevant observation on a point of law by a judge, but not binding.

objet d'art [Fr] (ob-zhay dar)
> A work of art.

objets d'occasion [Fr]
> Second-hand goods.

obscurum per obscurius [Lat]
> Trying to explain some obscure point by referring to something even more obscure.

ocha [Jap]
> Japanese tea. **Kocha** = Indian tea.

oderint dum metuant [Lat]
> Let them hate, so long as they fear.

odi et amo [Lat]
> I hate and I love; the 'love-hate' syndrome.

o dio! [It]
> Common Italian expression meaning, roughly, Good Lord! Good heavens! Blimey!

odium scholasticum [Lat]
>   The bitter disagreements among scholars.
>   **Odium theologicum** = acrimonious debate
>   between theologians. Similar for **odium
>   medicum** and **odium aestheticum**.

oeil-de-boeuf [Fr] (uhr-yuh-duh-burf)
>   Small round window in seventeenth- and
>   eighteenth-century French buildings.

œuf [Fr] (uhrf)
>   Egg. **oeufs brouillés** = scrambled eggs; **oeuf
>   dur** = hard-boiled egg; **oeuf poché** = poached
>   egg; **oeuf sur le plat** = fried egg; **une
>   omelette** = omelette.

œuvre [Fr] (urv-ruh)
>   The output of work, usually by a writer or
>   artist.

ogni medaglia ha il suo rovescio [It]
>   There are two sides to every medal (or coin).

ohne Wissen, ohne Sünde [Ger]
>   Without knowledge, without sin.

oleum addere camino [Lat]
>   Adding fuel to the fire.

¡olé!

This expression is now semi-anglicized and most
of us believe it means – approximately – 'Bravo!'
'Fantastic!' or some other shout of
encouragement during a performance.

But ¡olé! is rather more than that; it is,
especially at a flamenco performance, a deeply-
felt, emotional expression of appreciation,
generally shouted towards the end of a
movement and as much part of the show as the
music and dancing. It really means 'By God!'
and is perhaps closer to the biblical 'hallelujah!'
than to the meaning we have given it.

olio [Sp]
> Meat and vegetable stew. In Italian, ***olio*** = oil;
> ***olio d'oliva*** = olive oil.

omadhaun [Ir]
> A fool; an idiot.

omnem movere lapidem [Lat]
> Leave no stone unturned.

omnia ad Dei gloriam [Lat]
> All things to the glory of God.

omnia mors aequat [Lat]
> Death levels all.

omnia vincit amor [Lat] (om-nih-uh vin-kit ah-mor)
> Love conquers everything. ***Omnia vincit
> labor*** = labour conquers everything.

on dit [Fr] (or(n) dee)
> Literally: it is said. Gossip; rumour.

on parle français [Fr]
> French is spoken (here).

onus probandi [Lat]
> The burden of proof; it is up to the accuser to
> prove the allegation.

o omofilofilos [Gk]
> Homosexual. ***Haroomenos*** = gay, but in its
> traditional meaning of 'happy' or
> 'lighthearted'.

oozeri [Gk]
> Greek bar that serves ouzo and beer with
> ***mezés***, or snacks.

opéra bouffe [Fr] (op-ay-ruh boof)
> Comic opera.

opera buffa [It] (op-er-ruh boof-uh)
> Comic opera.

opere citato; ***op cit*** [Lat]
> In the work quoted; often seen in footnotes as
> the abbreviation ***op cit***.

opus Dei [Lat] (op-pus day-eh)
> The work of God.

ora et labora [Lat]
> Pray and work.

orbis terrarum [Lat]
>   The earth.
ordre du jour [Fr]
>   Order of the day; the agenda.
oshibori [Jap]
>   The moist cloth for wiping hands before a meal.

Oubykh and other dying languages

Oubykh, an unusual language with just three vowels but eighty consonants, was never an important language. It was, when first recorded, spoken by only 50,000 or so Caucasian people. Now there are none: the last Oubykh native speaker is believed to have died around 1989.

Dozens of languages are under threat. One is Ulithi, spoken on a remote Micronesian island by only 70 people. But even Ulithi has done better than Manx, now extinct, and Cornish, which losts its last native speaker a century or two ago. This did not, however, discourage schoolmaster Melville Bennetto from publishing the first novel in Cornish in 1984. 'I'm not expecting to make a fortune,' he said; there are only a couple of hundred people in the world who can understand it.

Are Welsh and Gaelic on the endangered list? With handsome government subsidies, Welsh is not only surviving but growing ever so slightly. So, for reasons hard to fathom, is the tiny pocket of some 80,000 Scots Gaelic speakers. But in Ireland, where about 1% of the population regularly use Gaelic, the picture is far from rosy. Despite Government encouragement and subsidies, even its most enthusiastic champions think it will disappear as a living language by the year 2000.

osteria [It]

   An inn in Italy.

O tempora! O mores! [Lat]

   (oh tem-por-uh, oh-moh-rays)

   Oh, what times! Oh, what manners! A
   traditional lament at falling standards of
   behaviour.

oui [Fr] (wee)

   Yes. The correct or authentically French
   pronunciation of ***oui*** is one of the most
   difficult of all to master.

outrance [Fr]

   Extreme; the last extremity; excess.

   outrancier = extremist.

outré [Fr] (oo-tray)

   Exaggerated; excessive; eccentric; extravagant.

ouvrage de longue haleine [Fr]

   Literally: a work of long breath. A long,
   sustained achievement.

P

pace [Lat] (pah-chay *also* pah-say)

   Preceding a person's name, it expresses polite
   disagreement about some point, but with
   apologies.

paella [Sp] (py-ELL-uh)

   A mixed dish of chicken, shellfish and perhaps
   other meats with rice.

pain [Fr]

   Bread, in various shapes and sizes: ***une***

baguette, une ficelle, un bâtard, un saucisson, etc. *Le pain grillé* = toast.

palazzo [It] (pah-LART-zoh)
Originally 'palace' but now any large mansion or building. *Palazzo municipale* = town hall.

palmam qui meruit ferat [Lat]
Let him bear the palm who has deserved it.

panem et circenses [Lat]
Bread and circuses (for the masses).

pannekoekhuisje [Dut]
Pancake house, serving up to fifty different kinds of these Dutch specialities.

paparazzo [It]
The ugly side of photography; 'sneak' news photographers. Plural: **paparazzi**.

papier [Fr] (pap-yay)
Paper. *Papier hygiénique* = toilet paper; *papier de soie* = tissue paper; *papier machine à écrire* = typing paper.

papillon [Fr]
Literally: butterfly. Colloquially, a parking ticket.

papillote [Fr]
Buttered paper used to wrap meat or fish which is then broiled.

para todo hay remedio sino para la muerte [Sp]
There is a remedy for everything except death.

parbleu! [Fr]
My God! Euphemism for *par Dieu*.

par excellence [Fr]
Pre-eminently; above all.

par exemple [Fr]
For instance.

pari mutuel [Fr]
A type of betting or lottery in which the winners share the available stake.

pari passu [Lat]
With equal speed; simultaneously.

paroles en l'air [Fr]
Idle words; pointless discussion.

partager le gâteau [Fr]
> To share the cake; split the takings.

partie carrée [Fr] (pah-tee kar-ray)
> A group of four people, customarily two couples.

parti pris [Fr] (par-tay PREE)
> A preconceived opinion.

parvenu [Fr]
> Someone who, becoming wealthy and having risen socially, is considered to be an unsuitable member of his or her new class. Feminine: ***parvenue***.

pas devant les enfants [Fr]
> (pah duh-vah(n) layz ah(n)-fah(n))
> Not in front of the children.

passer une nuit blanche [Fr]
> Literally: to pass a white night. To have a sleepless night.

passim [Lat]
> Here and there; in many places. Usually a footnote to show that a reference occurs throughout the book.

pasto [It]
> Meal. ***Anti-pasto*** = **hors d'œuvre**.

pastrami [Yid]
> Smoked, seasoned beef.

patchouli [Tamil]
> Fragrant oil and perfume from the leaves of the Pogostemon, an Asian tree.

pâté [Fr] (PAT-tay)
> Finely minced liver. ***Pâté de foie gras*** = paté of goose livers.

paterfamilias [Lat]
> The father; head of the household.

pâtisserie [Fr]
> French pastry shop.

pax Britannica [Lat]
> Peace imposed by British rule during the empire period.

Pas de deux (father of twins) and more fractured French

Like Liar's Latin, inventing Fractured French – coming up with new definitions for well-known phrases and sayings – is a pastime that's been around for generations, so don't be surprised if some of the examples below are a bit *passé*.

hors de combat – prostitute wrestlers
coup de grâce – lawnmower
tant mieux – spinster cat
entrechat – cat flap
après moi le déluge – April is the rainiest month
carte de visite – tourist bus
crêpe de chine – doggie droppings
tête-à-tête – a tight bra
tour de force – join the army, see the world
nostalgie de la boue – bring back those old horror films
lévee en masse – let them eat unleavened bread
rien n'arrive pour rien – when it rains it pours
vol-au-vent – wind in the stomach
eau de toilette – water from the loo
moi aussi – I am Australian

pax vobiscum! [Lat]
> Peace be with you!

paysage [Fr] (pay-zahzh)
> Landscape; landscape painting.

peccavi [Lat] (peh-KAR-vih)
> I have sinned. It is used light-heartedly as an apology. And as a pun; when British Army general Sir Charles Napier captured the Indian city of Sind he sent HQ a telegram which simply said *Peccavi*.

pedir peras al olmo [Sp]

> Don't try to find pears on an elm; don't expect
> the impossible.

peignoir [Fr] (pen-wahr)

> A woman's loose dressing-gown.

peintre de dimanche [Fr]

> A 'Sunday painter'; an amateur artist.

pelota [Sp]

> Game played by two players with small baskets
> strapped to their wrists to hurl a ball at a
> marked wall. See ***jai alai***, a similar game.

pendejo [Sp]

> Literally: pubic hair, but used colloquially to
> mean a fool; an idiot.

pensa molto, parla poco, e scrivi meno [It]

> Think much, talk little, and write less.

pensée [Fr] (pah(n)-say)

> A thought expressed in elegant writing.

pentimento [It]

> Revealing an addition or alteration made by an
> artist to a painting; revealing something
> previously hidden.

per diem [Lat]

> Each day.

père [Fr]

> Father.

perestroika [Rus] (peh-rih-STROY-kuh)

> The reform and restructuring of the political
> and economic systems of the former Soviet
> Union in the 1980s.

perfide Albion [Fr]

> Treacherous England. A traditional view held
> by the French.

per incuriam [Lat]

> By negligence; by oversight.

per procurationem; ***per pro***; ***pp*** [Lat]

> By proxy; by delegation to. The abbreviation
> ***pp*** is used by someone signing a letter or
> document on behalf of another.

Pidgin

Pidgin is a language formed from the vocabularies and grammars of other languages. English was a sort of pidgin many centuries ago when it was busy absorbing elements of Anglo-Saxon, Norse, Old French and Latin.

One of the most interesting pidgins today is Melanesian pidgin which, quaint as it looks and sounds, has become the lingua franca of Papua New Guinea (which has some 600 mother tongues), Solomon Islands, Vanuatu and other islands of Melanesia. It is also the official language of the Papua New Guinea parliament and has developed a grammatical structure. The number of people who use only pidgin, or who regard it as their mother tongue, is growing.

Unfortunately, to English eyes and ears pidgin seems little more than a comically corrupted language, but it has to earn full marks for vivid expression:

perscriptio in minibus tabellariorum est [Lat]
> The cheque is in the post.

per se [Lat] (pur say)
> In itself; by itself; essentially.

persona non grata [Lat]
> A person who is unacceptable or unwelcome.

pesca [It]
> Peach; but also fishing. **Pesce** = fish.

pescadinhas de rabo na boca [Port]
> Whiting served with the tails in their mouths.

péter [Fr]
> To fart. **Péter le feu** = to fart fire; to be full of energy.

ashes	*shit bilong faia*
moustache	*gras bilong maus* (mouth)
broken, ruined	*bagarap* (buggered-up)
house foundations	**ars** (arse = bottom) *bilong haus*
sexual intercourse	*push pushim*
Of no consequence	*samting nating* (something nothing)
hurricane lamp	*lam wokabout*

Just as graphic but more economical are these instructions for using western toilets (*Hao Yu Usim Kloset*):

1. *Putim daon sit blong kloset*
2. *Sidaon long maos blong bloset*
3. *Taem yu finis flusim kloset*
4. *Wasem han blong yu*

---

petit ami [Fr]
> Boy-friend. *Petite amie* = girl-friend.

petite bourgeoisie [Fr] (puh-teet boor-zhwah-zee)
> Lower middle classes. *Petit bourgeois* = a member of this class, usually used in a derogatory sense.

petits fours [Fr] (peh-tih FOOR)
> Fancily iced small cakes.

petits pois [Fr] (peh-tih-PWAH)
> Small, fresh green peas.

phrase toute faite [Fr]
> A cliché; a common phrase.

piac [Hung] (py-ut)
> Hungarian open market. The biggest and best-known is the ***Bosnyák téri piac*** in Budapest.

pibroch [Gael]
> A theme with variations for the Scottish bagpipe.

picante [Sp]
> Hot; highly peppered and spiced. ***Picanteria*** = restaurant specializing in hot food.

piccola morte [It]
> Literally: little death. An orgasm; a state of drug-induced oblivion.

pièce de résistance [Fr]
> The principal or special creation of an artist, performer or chef.

pied-à-terre [Fr] (pyay-dah-TAIR)
> Not a main residence, but usually a convenient town or city flat.

Pietà [It]
> The image of the Virgin Mary holding the dead body of Christ.

pijiu [Ch]
> Beer.

pila in area tua est [Lat]
> The ball is in your court.

pinxit [Lat]
> He or she painted it.

pique [Fr] (peek)
> A display of resentment and irritation.

piqué [Fr] (pee-kay)
> Ribbed fabric of cotton and silk.

piropos [Sp]
> The 'compliments' shouted to women by Hispanic males: the articulated and often explicit equivalent to the admiring whistle which a woman is supposed to ignore.

pis aller [Fr] (pee zah-lay)
> A last resort, in the absence of anything better.

piscem natare docere [Lat]
> Teaching a fish how to swim.

piscine [Fr]
> Swimming pool.

piste [Fr]
> A ski-run, slope or course.

pisto [Sp]
> Traditional Spanish dish of vegetables fried in olive oil. Do not confuse with ***pito***, which is slang for penis.

place au soleil, une [Fr]
> A place in the sun.

plage [Fr] (plahzh)
> Bathing beach.

plat du jour [Fr]
> A restaurant's dish of the day.

plein air [Fr]
> In the open air; a school of landscape painting.

plus ça change, plus c'est la même chose [Fr]
> (ploo sah shah(n)zh, ploo say lah mehm shohz)
> The more things change, the more they stay the same. Often shortened to ***plus ça change***.

Poetic licence

In a magazine travel article on Australia, the well-known English poet commissioned to write it commented on the cry of the Western Australian Twenty-eight parrot, so named, he said, because its call sounded like 'twenty-eight, twenty-eight'.

Either the poetic ear was on holiday or something was lost in translation. The bird was, in fact, first described by a French ornithologist who reported, correctly, that its call sounded like ***vingt-huit, vingt-huit*** (vah(n)t-weet, vah(n)t-weet), which, of course, means twenty-eight, twenty-eight in French!

---

poi [Hawaiian]
>A dish made from fermented taro root.

pointillism [Fr]
>Style of painting, made famous by Seurat, which uses multi-coloured dots to achieve an impressionistic effect.

polenta [It]
>Thick maize porridge.

polizia [It]]
>Italian police. ***Metropolitani*** = Municipal police; ***Corpo della Pubblica Sicurezza*** = Public police; ***Pubblica Sicurezza*** and ***Carabinieri*** = Military police; ***Guardia di Finanza*** = Customs police; ***Polizia Giudiziaria*** = Criminal Investigation Dept; ***polizia stradale*** = traffic police; ***vigili notturni*** = private security guards.

pommes frites [Fr] (pohm-freet)
>French fries; chip potatoes.

portière [Fr]
>The anti-draught curtain behind a door.

posada [Sp]
>Spanish inn.

poste restante [Fr] (post RES-tah(n)t)
>Section of a post office that keeps mail for collection.

post meridiem; ***p.m.*** [Lat]
>After noon; afternoon.

post nubila, Phoebus [Lat]
>After clouds, the sun.

post obitum [Lat]
>After death.

post scriptum; **postscript**; ***PS*** [Lat]
>An addition or note added below the signature.

potage [Fr]
>Soup.

pot-au-feu [Fr]
>Boiled beef in broth.

pot-pourri [Fr] (poh-poo-ree)

    A miscellany; a medley; a mixed collection; specifically a mixture of dried, fragrant rose and other flower petals.

pourboire [Fr] (poor-bwahr)

    A tip; gratuity.

pour épater les bourgeois [Fr]

    To shock the middle classes.

pourquoi? [Fr]

    Why?

pour rire [Fr]

    In fun; not to be taken seriously.

précieuse [Fr] (pray-syurz)

    Precious; affected.

préciosité [Fr] (pray-sios-ih-tay)

    Extreme affectation.

prego [It] (pray-goh)

    The equivalent of 'don't mention it', said to someone who thanks you.

prêt-à-porter [Fr]

    Ready to wear.

prima facie [Lat] (pree-mah fay-sih)

    At first sight; in law, using available but not necessarily complete or tested evidence to arrive at a conclusion.

primus inter pares [Lat]

    First among equals; having precedence but only equal authority.

pris sur le fait [Fr]

    Caught in the act.

prix d'ami [Fr]

    A 'special price' for a friend.

prix fixe [Fr]

    An inclusive fixed price, usually for a meal.

pro bono publico [Lat]

    For the public good.

profanum vulgus [Lat]

    The herd; the common multitude.

pro forma [Lat]
> According to procedure; as a matter of form.
> A ***pro forma*** invoice is one issued before
> purchase and delivery of the goods.

pro rata [Lat]
> In proportion; proportionally.

pro rege et patria [Lat]
> For king and country.

prosit! [Lat]
> Good health! German and other languages have
> it as ***prost!***; the Dutch is ***proost!***

pro tempore; ***pro tem*** [Lat]
> For the time being; temporarily.

prudens futuri [Lat]
> Thinking of the future.

psaria [Gk]
> Fish. ***Psarotaverna*** = fish restaurant.

psistaria [Gk]
> Restaurant specializing in charcoal grills.

puîné [Fr]
> Younger. ***Puisné*** = Old French, meaning 'born
> later' from which is derived the class of judges
> known as puisne judges, i.e. of lower rank.

puissance [Fr] (pwee-sah(n)s)
> Show-jumping competition to test a horse's
> ability over a series of close high jumps.

pukka [Hindi]
> Properly done; genuine.

puta [Sp]
> Whore, and a common vulgarism. ***Hijo de
> puta*** is one of the top ten Hispanic insults.

putsch [Ger] (pootch)
> A violent overthrow of authority.

Q

qarwah [Arab]
> Coffee.

Quai d'Orsay [Fr] (kay-DOR-say)
> The French Foreign Ministry.

qualche volta è virtù tacere il vero [It]
> Sometimes it is a virtue to conceal the truth.

qualis vita, finis ita [Lat]
> As in life, so is the end.

Quartier Latin [Fr]
> The Paris bohemian south bank area.

quattrocento [It]
> The fifteenth century; art of that period.

que besa sus pies [Sp]
> Literally: who kisses your feet. Shortened to **QBSP** it is a writer's fond sign-off in a letter to a woman.

quenelle [Fr]
> Seasoned, fried meat or fish balls.

quequette; kiquette [Fr]
> Vulgar slang for penis.

querelle d'Allemand [Fr]
> German quarrel, i.e. an uncalled-for quarrel.

que sais-je? [Fr]
> What do I know?

que sera sera [Sp] (kay suh-RAR suh-RAR)
> What will be will be.

que ta chemise ne sache ta guise [Fr]
> Don't let even your cap know what thoughts it covers.

Quebec's tongue troopers

The French-speaking holdout in Canada is Quebec where, since 1976, Bill 101, the province's French language charter, and Bill 178, the sign law, have banned all languages other than French from Quebec life. The Draconian language laws are administered by the *Commission de Surveillance de la Langue Française*, unpopularly known as the 'vocabulary constabulary' or the 'tongue troopers'.

The laws have been only partly successful and are generally scorned, especially by the 800,000 Quebecois who are anglophones. One town – named Buckingham after its English counterpart – was fined for defying an order to remove the words 'Town Hall' from its town hall. Quebec's efforts to control the language of the people seems, like similar efforts in the past, to be doomed: English-speaking people are leaving, the birth-rate of the francophone population is falling, and fewer immigrants are arriving.

quid pro quo [Lat]
> Something for something; an equitable exchange.

quieta non movere [Lat]
> Let sleeping dogs lie.

qui m'aime aime mon chien [Fr]
> Who loves me loves my dog.

quinta [Sp]
> In Spain, originally a country house, but now usually a suburban villa.

quis custodiet ipsos custodes? [Lat]
>Who will guard the guards?

qui s'excuse s'accuse [Fr]
>He who makes excuses for himself accuses
himself.

Quittung [Ger]
>Receipt.

qui vive [Fr] (kee-veev)
>The alert.

quod erat demonstrandum; ***QED*** [Lat]
>That which was to be demonstrated or proved.

quod vide; ***q.v.*** [Lat]
>Which see. The abbreviation ***q.v.*** is used to
advise readers to consult other references on the
subject.

quo vadis? [Lat]
>Whither goest thou?

R

Rache trägt keine Frucht [Ger]
>Revenge brings no fruit.

radschlagen [Ger]
>To perform a gymnastic cartwheel. ***Die
Düsseldorfer Radschläger*** = the cartwheel
performances on the Königsstraße, well known
to tourists.

raffreddore [It]
>The common cold in Italy; colloquially known
as catching a ***freddo***.

ragoût [Fr] (rah-goo)
>Highly seasoned stew.

raison d'état [Fr]
> Reason(s) of state; for the state's security.

raison d'être [Fr] (ray-zoh(n) det-ruh)
> Reason for existing.

râle de la mort [Fr]
> Death rattle.

Ramadan [Arab]
> The religious thirty-day sunrise-to-sunset fast in the ninth month of the Muslim year.

rapporteur [Fr]
> Someone directed to investigate and to submit a report on the findings.

rapprochement [Fr] (rah-PROSH-mah(n))
> A coming together; establishing or re-establishing friendly relations.

rara avis [Lat] (rah-ruh AY-vis)
> Literally: rare bird. Something or someone most unusual and rarely encountered.

Rasthaus [Ger]
> Small motel by main roads and the ***Autobahnen*** in which travellers can rest for a few hours.

ratatouille [Fr] (rat-ah-TWEE)
> Fried and stewed vegetable casserole.

Rathaus [Ger] (RAH-tows)
> German town hall.

Ratskeller [Ger]
> Upmarket restaurant, as distinct from the ***Gastkeller*** where drinkers are likely to outnumber diners.

rav [Heb]
> Rabbi.

Realpolitik [Ger]
> Politics based on practicalities and opportunism rather than ideals and morals.

rebozo [Sp]
> Shawl worn by Hispanic women over their heads and shoulders.

réchauffé [Fr] (ray-shoh-fay)
> Warmed up leftovers; anything rehashed from old, stale materials.

recherché [Fr] (ruh-SHAIR-shay)
> Refined and rare; obscure.

réclame [Fr] (ray-KLAHM)
> Self-advertisement; publicity-seeking; a talent for notoriety.

reculer pour mieux sauter [Fr]
> A strategic retreat in order to make a more effective advance.

rédacteur [Fr]
> Publishing editor. **Rédaction** = editing.

Reden ist Silber, Schweigen ist Gold [Ger]
> Speech is silver, silence is gold.

reductio ad absurdum [Lat]
> To prove the falsity of a proposition by demonstrating that its logical conclusion is absurd.

règlement [Fr]
> The rule or regulation. **Il faut agir selon les règlements** = you must conform to the rules.

Reich [Ger] (ry-kh)
> German empire or state. Specifically, the **First Reich** (962–1806 or Bismarck's empire of 1871–1919); **Second Reich** (Weimar Republic, 1919–1933); **Third Reich** (Nazi Germany, 1933–1945).

relais routier [Fr] (reh-lay root-yay)
> Roadside restaurant and rest-place used by travellers and lorry drivers.

relata refero [Lat]
> I tell it as it was told to me.

religieuse [Fr]
> Nun. **Religieux** = monk or brother.

remonte-pente [Fr]
> Ski-lift.

rémoulade [Fr]
> Herb mayonnaise sauce for salads.

renaissance [Fr]
>Rebirth; revival. **Renaissance** = classical revival in the fifteenth–sixteenth centuries.

renkött [Swed]
>Reindeer.

renommé [Fr]
>Celebrated; famous.

rentier [Fr] (rah(n)t-yay)
>Someone who lives off investments or has independent means.

repas maigre [Fr]
>Vegetarian (meatless) meal.

repêchage [Fr] (reh-peh-sharzh)
>A heat in a contest in which runners-up in previous heats compete for a place in the final.

répondez, s'il vous plaît; **RSVP** [Fr] (ray-poh(n)-day, seel voo play)
>Reply if you please.

requiescat in pace; **RIP** [Lat] (rek-wih-ES-kat in pah-chay)
>May he/she rest in peace.

retroussé [Fr] (ruh-TROO-say)
>Turned up nose.

revanche [Fr] (ruh-VANSH)
>Literally: revenge. **Revanchisme** = policy of retaliation to regain something lost.

réveillon [Fr]
>French Christmas and New Year's celebrations usually involving meals and drinks after midnight.

revenons à nos moutons [Fr]
>Literally: Let's return to our sheep. Let's return to the subject; let's get back to the point.

rex non potest peccare [Lat]
>The king can do no wrong.

ride bene chi ride l'ultimo [It]
>He laughs best who laughs last.

ridere in stomacho [Lat]
>To laugh up your sleeve.

Rhyming slang

The Times's grammar guru, Philip Howard, tells of an exchange he had with a news vendor on the London Underground. 'How are you?' he asked. He was told: 'Cold – this perishin' wind's blowin' straight up me plaster!' Plaster? Eventually Howard traced it back: **plaster = Plaster of Paris = arris = Aristotle = bottle = bottle and glass = arse**.

That's Cockney rhyming slang *in extremis*. Most of it is simply one rhyme removed, as with these well-known examples: **titfer = tit for tat = hat; boracic = boracic lint = skint** (or **broke**); **frog = frog and toad = road; syrup = syrup of fig = wig**.

Rhyming slang sometimes takes on the qualities of a foreign language, in that you can't understand it. Here are a few examples that can have you guessing:

barnet = Barnet Fair = hair
harvey = Harvey Nichols = pickles
linen = linen draper = paper = newspaper
Kate and Sidney = steak and kidney
sweeny = Sweeny Todd = the Flying Squad = detectives
oxo = Oxo cube = tube = Underground

The more streetwise readers will need no help with **fun and frolics, khyber,** and **orchestras**.

rijstafel [Dut] (rays-tah-fel)
    Indonesian banquet based on rice with a variety of vegetables and meats.
rincer les yeux [Fr]
    'Eyewash': colloquial for an admiring gaze at an attractive object, usually a woman.

ripopée [Fr]
>Dregs; slops; what's left.

rira bien qui rira le dernier [Fr]
>He laughs best who laughs last.

rive gauche [Fr] (reev gohsh)
>The left bank of the Seine in Paris; the Latin Quarter.

rivière [Fr]
>Multi-stringed necklace of precious stones.

robe de chambre [Fr] (rohb duh shah(n)-bruh)
>Dressing-gown.

roman-à-clef [Fr] (roh-mah(n)-ah-klay)
>A novel which describes real events and has real people as characters.

romanesco; *romano* [It]
>The dialect of Rome.

roman-fleuve [Fr]
>Series of novels about one group or family.

romanista [It]
>A Rome Football Club supporter. The other Roman team is the Lazio FC or the *biancoazzurri*, whose supporters are called *laziale*.

rompiscatole [It]
>Literally: ball-breaker. Vulgar for a bore, pest or nuisance.

rondelet; *rondelette* [Fr]
>Plump; chubby; a well-rounded person.

rondine [It]
>A swallow. *Una rondine non fa primavera* = one swallow doesn't make a spring.

Rosh Hashanah [Heb] (rohsh hah-SHAH-nuh)
>Jewish New Year.

rôti [Fr] (roh-tee)
>In cooking, to roast; roasted food.

roublard [Fr]
>Cunning; a sharp character.

roué [Fr] (roo-ay)
>A lecherous, debauched male.

roux [Fr] (roo)
> Blend of butter or other fat and flour, used as the basis for sauces.

rusé [Fr] (roo-zay)
> Wily; tricky; cunning.

rus in urbe [Lat] (roos in UR-bih)
> Bringing the country to the city; the creation of rural atmosphere in a town.

Russian

Modern Russian is absorbing English words and terms at a breathtaking rate and the language is now so heavily invaded by English jargon, slang and *tekhnologiya* that the Western visitor can make passable progress without recourse to the native tongue. Which, perhaps, is just as well: with its upside-down-reversed-looking alphabet, complex grammar and palatal pronunciation, Russian can't be an easy language to master.

But with so many English-flavoured words in the modern vocabulary it's almost possible to read a Russian newspaper, where you'll come across **rok** (rock), **dzhaz** (jazz), **dzinsi** (jeans), **kasety** (casette), **shuz** (shoes), **vash** (watch) and even a **finalny match of basketbolny**. What was once a **vychislitelnaya mashina** is now a **kompyuter**. Efficiency is **effektivnost** and gangsters are **gangstery**. And striptease is, surprise, surprise – **striptiz**.

---

ryokan [Jap]
> Traditional Japanese inns in which guests can experience local food and customs.

S

sacré bleu! [Fr]
    Curse it! Confound it!

sain et sauf [Fr]
    Safe and sound.

salaam [Arab] (sah-LAHM)
    Peace. A Muslim salutation.

salaud, un [Fr] (sah-LOH)
    Bastard; swine; sod, etc. **Petite salaud** = little
    bastard.

salata horiatiki [Gk]
    Greek salad.

salière [Fr]
    Salt-cellar.

salle à manger [Fr] (sal-ah-mah(n) zhay)
    Dining-room.

salle d'attente [Fr] (sal dah-tah(n)t)
    Waiting-room.

salope [Fr]
    A bitch.

saltimbanque [Fr]
    A quack; a crook.

saltimbocca [It]
    Herbed dish of folded veal and prosciutto.

salvete [Lat]
    Welcome! Greetings!

salvo pudore [Lat]
    Without offence to modesty.

samadhi [Hindi]
    An ultimate trance-like state in yoga.

san [Jap]

> The word you add to all Japanese surnames (which in Japan are written first: with Harawa Keiko, Harawa is the surname; Keiko is the given name) which is the all-purpose equivalent of Mr, Mrs and Ms.

sanctum sanctorum [Lat]

> The holy of holies; a private sanctum.

sang froid [Fr] (sah(n) frwah)

> Composure; calmness; self-possession.

sans [Fr]

> Without.

sans blague [Fr] (sah(n) blahg)

> Without joking; seriously.

sansculotte [Fr] (sah(n)-koo-LOT)

> Originally a poor revolutionary; any republican extremist.

sans doute [Fr]

> Without doubt.

sans façon [Fr] (sah(n) fah-soh(n))

> Unceremoniously; brusquely.

sans gêne [Fr] (sah(n) shehn)

> Disregard for politeness; when someone is offending without realizing it.

sans peur et sans reproche [Fr]

> Without fear and above reproach.

sans prétensions [Fr]

> Unpretentious; unaffected.

santé [Fr] (sah(n)-tay)

> Good health.

Sartor Resartus [Lat]

> The tailor mended.

sashimi [Jap]

> Varieties of raw fish served as a meal.

satis eloquentiae, sapientiae parum [Lat]

> Abounding eloquence, scant wisdom.

saucisse; ***saucisson*** [Fr]

> The former is an uncooked sausage; the latter is a cooked sausage for eating cold.

A *saucière* of sauces

The great French cook Alexis Soyer once wrote that 'Sauces are to cookery what grammar is to language'. This was about the time that England was reviled as a 'nation with one sauce' but since then things – and sauces – have moved on a bit and the average British diner today is familiar with at least a few of them. Are you?

Sauce à la menthe	mint
Sauce Allemande	butter, flour, lemon juice, nutmeg
Sauce au beurre	butter
Sauce aux câpres	capers
Sauce aux cornichons	brown sauce with gherkins
Sauce béarnaise	egg yolks, butter, vinegar and tarragon
Sauce béchamel	white roux with seasoning – the foundation of many other sauces

säufer [Ger]
> Drunkard; alcoholic. *Er säuft wie ein Loch* = someone who 'drinks like a fish'.

Sauregurkenzeit [Ger]
> Literally: pickled gherkin time – a period when nothing is happening in business or politics. Known elsewhere as the 'silly season'.

savoir-faire [Fr] (sav-wahr FAIR)
> Polished; tactful; having the ability to do the right thing when required.

Sauce bordelaise	with claret, shallots, seasoning
Sauce bretonne	simple egg and butter sauce
Sauce espagnole	thick basic brown sauce
Sauce financière	with madeira or sherry
Sauce génoise	fish stock, anchovy butter, claret
Sauce hollandaise	warmed egg yolks, butter, lemon
Sauce meunière	butter, parsley, lemon juice
Sauce mousseline	*sauce hollandaise* with whipped cream
Sauce régence	fish stock and Marsala wine
Sauce tartare	for fish and seafood
Sauce tournée	with onions and mushrooms
Sauce valois	egg yolks, vinegar, shallots
Sauce velouté	a variation of bechamel
Sauce zwetschen	prunes, port, lemon juice, cinnamon

sayonara [Jap]
> Goodbye.

sbirro [It]
> Colloquial for Italian policeman.

scappatella [It]
> Flirtation; brief extra-marital relationship.

schadenfreude [Ger] (SHAH-den-froy-duh)
> A fashionable word of the 1990s meaning taking malicious pleasure from another's misfortune. Until recently, as a non-anglicized word it carried a capital *S*.

schemozzle [Yid] (shih-MOZZ-ul)
> A mix-up; mess; argument.

Schickse [Ger]
> Tart; trollop.

schifo [It]
> Disgust. ***Mi far schifo*** = it makes me sick! A widely used colloquial word for complaining.

Schlafen Sie wohl! [Ger]
> Sleep well!

Schlager [Ger]
> Pop song; a musical hit.

schlemiel [Yid] (shluh-MEEL)
> A simple person, usually a man, who has the best intentions but no luck; unlucky but uncomplaining.

schlep; ***shlep*** [Yid]
> To drag or carry with effort.

Schlimmbesserung [Ger]
> An improvement that makes things worse.

schlock [Yid]
> Cheap; inferior; rubbish; in bad taste.

Schloss [Ger]
> A German castle; a country estate.

schmaltz; ***shmaltz*** [Yid]
> Sugary sentimentality.

schmuck; ***shmuk*** [Yid]
> Someone who always does the wrong thing.

schnorrer [Yid] (shnor-ruh)
> Beggar.

schön [Ger]
> Beautiful; nice. ***Schönheitsfarm*** = health farm.

Schrecklichkeit [Ger]
> The deliberate perpetration of atrocities to subjugate a population.

schuss [Ger] (shooss)
> In skiing, a straight fast downhill run.

schwarz [Ger]
> Black, but like the English term 'black market'

can also mean 'illegal': ***schwarzarbeiten*** =
earning extra untaxed income;
schwarzsehen = to have a TV receiver
without a licence.

scientiae causa [Lat]
> To carry out difficult or painful experiments in
> the cause of science.

scippo [It]
> Bag-snatching – unfortunately a common
> occurrence in Italian cities. ***Scippatore*** = bag-
> snatcher.

scirocco; sirocco [It]] (sih-ROK-koh)
> The wind that blows from the Sahara, north to
> Italy: warm, oppressive and sandy.

scudetto [It]
> ***Lo Scudetto*** = Italian First Division Soccer
> Championship for the tricolour shield. One of
> the top ***Serie A*** teams is AC Milan whose ***tifosi***
> (supporters) fill Milan's San Siro stadium.

sculpsit [Lat]
> He (or she) sculpted it.

séance d'essais [Fr]
> A preliminary run by racing cars before a race
> to familiarize drivers with the course.

se battre contre des moulins [Fr]
> To battle against windmills.

secrétaire [Fr]
> An enclosed writing desk with a drop writing
> table, drawers and pigeon-holes.

securus judicat orbis terrarum [Lat]
> The judgement of the whole world can't be
> wrong.

s'emmerder [Fr]
> Colloquial: to be bored.

semper fidelis [Lat] (sem-per fih-DAY-lis)
> Always faithful.

Senhor; ***Senhora***; ***Senhorita*** [Port]
>Portuguese form of address for a man, married
>woman and unmarried woman respectively.

Señor; ***Señora***; ***Señorita*** [Sp]
>The Spanish addresses for a man, married
>woman and unmarried woman respectively.

sensu abscaeno [Lat]
>To take the obscene meaning of a word or
>statement.

Serenissima, La [It]
>Colloquial for the Republic of Venice.

sérieux [Fr]
>Serious; sincere; earnest.

se saouler la gueule [Fr]
>Vulgar for 'to get drunk'.

sesquipedalia verba [Lat]
>Horace's pun 'Words of a foot and a half';
>extremely long words.

seul [Fr]
>Alone; single. ***Tout seul*** = by oneself; ***un
>homme seul*** = a lonely man; ***seul à seul*** =
>tete-à-tete.

sgian-dhu [Gael]
>The dirk or knife carried in a Scottish
>Highlander's sock.

shaay [Arab]
>Tea.

shabash! [Hindi]
>Well done! Excellent!

shabat [Heb]
>The Sabbath.

shalom [Heb] (shuh-LOM)
>Peace; hello. A common Jewish salutation.

shekel [Heb]
>Main Israeli unit of currency, divided into 100
>**agorot** (singular **agora**).

shikker [Yid]
>A drunk. ***Shikkered*** = to be drunk.

shiksa [Yid]
> A non-Jewish girl; a Jewish girl by birth but non-practising.

shinkansen [Jap]
> Bullet train. The **hikari** is the express; the **kodama** is the high-speed stopping train.

shtik [Yid]
> A routine unique to a performer; a special act.

shuk; **suq** [Arab]
> Open market-place. Usually spelt **souk**.

sic [Lat]
> Thus written; thus said. Used in brackets [**sic**] to indicate that a word, possibly misspelt, or a statement, possibly inaccurate, is being reproduced or quoted exactly.

sic semper tyrannis [Lat]
> Thus be the fate of tyrants. Uttered by Abraham Lincoln's assassin in 1865.

sic transit gloria mundi [Lat]
> Thus passes the glory of the world; worldly attainments are soon forgotten.

Sieg heil! [Ger] (zeek HY-uhl)
> Hail to victory: the infamous Nazi salute, accompanied by the raised arm.

si fractum non sit, noli id reficere [Lat]
> If it isn't broken, don't fix it.

Signore; **Signora**; **Signorina** [It]
> Italian forms of address for a man, married woman and an unmarried woman respectively.

si jeunesse savait, si vieillesse pouvait [Fr]
> If youth but knew, if age but could.

s'il vous plaît [Fr] (see-voo-play)
> If you please.

si parla italiano [It]
> Italian spoken here.

simpatico [It]
> Pleasant; likeable; nice. **Antipatico** = unpleasant; **simpaticone** = likeable person.

simplicissimus [Lat]

>A simple-minded man who, despite being
>exploited by others, is philosophical about his
>situation.

simpliste [Fr]

>Simplistic; too simple to be credible.

sine die [Lat] (see-nay dee-ay)

>Without a day or date being fixed.

sine qua non [Lat] (see-nay kwah non)

>An essential requirement or condition.

Sinn Fein [Ir] (shin-fayn)

>Irish republican movement founded in 1905;
>the political arm of the Irish Republican Army
>(IRA).

sit venia verbis [Lat]

>Pardon my words.

si vis pacem, para bellum [Lat]

>If you desire peace, prepare for war.

skål; ***skoal*** (Swed)

>Cheers! Good health!

sláinte [Gael]

>Good health!

smörgåsbord [Swed]

>Traditional spread of food from salt fish, meats
>and salads through to hot dishes and cheese
>from which diners help themselves.

snobisme [Fr]

>Following intellectual fashions.

Sociedad Anónima; ***SA*** [Sp]

>Corporation equivalent to the English '&
>Company Limited' or '& Co Ltd.'

Société Anonyme; ***SA*** [Fr]

>French equivalent of the English '& Company
>Limited' or '& Co Ltd'.

Société Nationale des Chemins de Fer; ***SNCF*** [Fr]

>The French nationalized railway system.

soi-disant [Fr] (swah-dee-zah(n))

>So-called; self-styled.

soigné [Fr] (swahn-yay)
> Elegantly groomed.

soirée [Fr] (swah-ray)
> An evening gathering where guests talk and listen or dance to music.

---

soixante-neuf [Fr] (swas-ah(n)t-nuhrf)
This little number is known to most schoolchildren well before their first French lessons. Or even history lessons:

Old Louis Quatorze was hot stuff,
He tired of that game, Blind Man's Bluff,
    Up-ended his mistress,
    Kissed hers while she kissed his,
And thus taught the world *soixante-neuf*.

---

soldi [It]
> Money. *Senza un soldo* = broke.

son et lumière [Fr] (sohn ay loom-yair)
> Literally: sound and light. An evening entertainment staged outside an historic building, with words, music and lighting effects to illustrate its history.

sortes Biblicae [Lat] (sor-tez BIB-lih-ki)
> Prophesying by opening the Bible at any page and selecting the passage the eye first sees; this passage is prophetic. The same is done with the works of Virgil and Homer.

sotto voce [It] (sot-toh VOH-chay)
> In an undertone.

sottogoverno [It]
> Italian political patronage whereby the relatives of successful candidates and supporters of victorious parties share government posts, jobs, contracts and cash.

souk [Arab]
> See *shuk*.

soupçon [Fr] (soop-soh(n))
> A tiny amount; a dash.

soutane [Fr] (soo-tahn)
> Roman Catholic priest's cassock.

spalpeen [Ir]
> Itinerant worker; layabout; rascal.

A Spanish conundrum

A young Spanish woman entered a London men's clothing store and, knowing no English, and since the staff knew no Spanish, had great difficulty in making herself understood.

However, in a flash of inspiration, one of the salesmen began pointing to the various articles of clothing. After several minutes he appeared to have hit on the desired item.

'*¡Eso si que es!*' the young woman exclaimed, using a Spanish expression that means 'That's just what I wanted'!

The sales staff, who were under the impression she knew no English at all, were not amused by the time-wasting. 'Why didn't you spell it out for me at the start?' the angry salesman asked her.

What was the item of clothing the woman wanted?

(*Answer on page 164*)

Spätzündung [Ger]
> Literally: retarded ignition. *Er hat Spätzündung* = he's slow on the uptake.

spécialité de la maison [Fr]
> The chef's special dish at a particular restaurant.

sperat infestis, metuit secundis [Lat]
> He hopes in adversity, fears in prosperity.

splendide mendax [Lat]
> Telling a lie for a good cause.

splitterfasernackt [Ger]
> Absolutely naked; starkers.

sprezzatura [It]
> The bravura or effortless technique of a great artist.

spurlos versunken [Ger]
> Sunk or vanished without trace.

Stammplatz [Ger]
> A favourite place.

stamppot [Dut]
> Traditional potato and vegetable hash, usually served with bacon and sausages.

Stasi [Ger]
> Abbreviation of *Staatssicherheitspolizei*, Secret Police.

status quo [Lat]
> Existing or prevailing state of affairs.

stet [Lat]
> Let it stand. Used in typography to indicate that an alteration is to be ignored.

stet fortuna domus [Lat]
> May the fortunes of the house endure.

Stiefel [Ger]
> The peculiar large boot- or foot-shaped glass tankard filled with beer and passed from drinker to drinker at parties. The idea is to drink without the beer gurgling or surging out over the drinker.

stoep [Dut] (stooph)
> The front verandah of a house.

Storbritannien [Swed]
> Great Britain.

Stundenhotel [Ger]
> At first sight a hostel for students but in fact a disorderly house or brothel.

Sturm und Drang [Ger] (shterm oont drahng)
>   Literally: storm and stress. Originally an over-
>   heated German literary style; now an
>   expression for tumult and extravagant passion.

style champêtre [Fr]
>   In painting, idyllic pastoral scenes.

sua cuique sunt vitia [Lat]
>   Every man has his vices.

sub judice [Lat] (sub JOO-dih-say)
>   Under judicial consideration; as yet undecided
>   by a court.

sub rosa [Lat]
>   In secret; in strict confidence.

suburbio [Sp]
>   In Hispanic countries, the run-down shanty
>   areas on the outskirts of cities.

succès de scandale [Fr] (sook-say duh skah(n)-darl)
>   Success of a play or book due to its scandalous
>   nature.

succès d'estime [Fr] (sook-say deh-steem)
>   Success of a play or book due to critical, rather
>   than public, acclaim.

succès fou [Fr] (sook-say foo)
>   A mad, wild, brilliant success.

suggestio falsi [Lat]
>   Misrepresentation without actually lying.

sui generis [Lat]
>   Of its own kind; unique.

summa cum laude [Lat] (sum-uh kum LOW-day)
>   With the highest distinction; with the utmost
>   praise.

Sunna [Arab]
> The body of Islamic law that orthodox Muslims accept as based on the words and acts of Mohammed.

supercherie [Fr]
> A hoax or fraud.

supermarché [Fr]
> Supermarket. A really large supermarket is called *un hypermarché*.

suppressio veri [Lat]
> Suppression of the truth; concealment of the facts.

supra vires [Lat]
> Beyond a person's powers.

Sûreté [Fr] (syur-uh-tay)
> French police criminal investigation department. *Sûreté Générale* = French equivalent of Britain's Scotland Yard.

sushi [Jap]
> Small parcels of raw fish wrapped in boiled rice.

suum cuique [Lat]
> To each his own.

Sverige [Swed]
> Sweden. *Svensk* = Swedish; *Svenska* – Swedish language.

Systemzwang [Ger]
> A compulsion for system and order.

szálloda [Hung]
> Hotel. Smaller establishments, similar to bed and breakfasts, are *panzió* and *fogadó*. Chalet-type hotels for group acommodation are called *túristaszálló*.

T

tableau vivant [Fr] (tab-loh vih-vah(n))
A scene or painting represented by a posed group of still, silent people.

table d'hôte [Fr] (tab-luh doht)
Fixed price restaurant menu with minimal choice.

tabula rasa [Lat]
Literally: scraped tablet. A fresh surface ready to receive a new impression; a fresh mind open to receive information; an opportunity for a fresh start.

taedium vitae [Lat]
Weariness of life.

Tageblätter [Ger]
Newspapers.

tai chi chuan [Ch]
Variety of Chinese unarmed combat.

taille [Fr]
Your measurements (height, waist, size) as seen on European garment labels. For shoes, socks, tights and gloves, size is expressed by *la pointure*.

tal para cual [Sp]
Tit for tat (also *taz a taz*).

tamal; tamales [Sp]
Hash of maize and meat wrapped in a leaf.

Tannenbaum [Ger]
Christmas tree; pine tree.

tant mieux [Fr] (tah(n) myur)
So much the better.

tant pis [Fr] (tah(n) pee)
> So much the worse.

Taoiseach [Ir] (tee-shak)
> Prime Minister of the Irish Republic.

tapas [Sp]
> Snacks served with drinks; also called
> ***aperitivos***.

tapis [Fr] (tah-pee)
> A rug. ***Un tapis de bain*** = bathmat.

taramasalata [Gk]
> Pâté of cod's roe.

tashinamu [Jap]
> Devotion to a cause with little likelihood of
> recognition or success.

taverna [Gk]
> Greek restaurant where wine is served.

Taxe à la Valeur Ajoutée; ***TVA*** [Fr]
> VAT or Value Added Tax.

tchin tchin [Fr]
> Cheers!

Te Deum [Lat]
> Thee, God, we praise. Hymn of praise and for
> giving thanks.

teishok [Jap]
> A fairly standard set meal of rice, soup, pickles
> and a selected dish. ***Tonkats teishok*** = set
> meal with pork as the main dish.

tel père, tel fils [Fr]
> Like father, like son.

témoignage [Fr]
> Factual, unprejudiced testimony.

tempora mutantur et nos mutamur in illis [Lat]
> Times change and we change with them.

tempura [Jap]
> Crispy deep-fried seafood and vegetables.

tempus fugit [Lat]
> Time flies.

tendresse [Fr]
> Affection; fondness; tenderness.

tep-panyaki [Jap]
>Beef and vegetables grilled at the table.

terminus vita [Lat]
>Death; end of life.

terra firma [Lat]
>Firm ground; solid earth; a land mass.

terra incognita [Lat] (teh-ruh in-KOG-nih-tuh)
>Unknown or unexplored regions.

tête-à-tête [Fr] (teht-ah-teht)
>A private conversation between two people.

Thai

Visitors to a temple in Bangkok are confronted with a sign which reads, 'It is forbidden to enter a woman'. Then, in smaller letters: 'Even a foreigner if dressed as a man'.

Thailand offers its millions of tourist visitors not only exotic food but also food for thought. For what would a diner make of 'Good Woman pullit' on the menu of a Bangkok restaurant? Or of a novelty doll sold by souvenir shops 'which laughs while you throw up'? Who ever said the Thais don't have a sense of humour?

---

tibi gratias agimus quod nihil fumas [Lat]
>Thank you for not smoking.

tibi seris, tibi metis [Lat]
>As ye sow, so shall ye reap.

tic douloureux [Fr]
>A neuralgic affliction characterized by twitching facial muscles.

tiens! [Fr]
>Really! You don't say ! Well, hullo!

timbres-poste [Fr]
>Postage stamps.

timeo Danaos et dona ferentes [Lat]
>I fear the Greeks even when they bear gifts.

timor addidit alas [Lat]
>Fear gave him wings (Virgil).

tirez le rideau, la farce est jouée [Fr]
>Bring down the curtain, the farce is over.

todo cae en el dedo malo [Sp]
>Everything falls on the injured finger.

tokaji [Hun] (toh-KAY)
>Hungarian wine made from the furmint grape. The famous sweet wines are ***Aszu*** and ***Aszu Eszencia***.

tonto [Sp]
>Stupid; silly. ***Una tonteria*** = a stupid thing.

topi; ***topee*** [Hindi]
>Sun hat; pith helmet.

Torah [Heb]
>The scroll on which Jewish law is written.

tortilla [Sp] (tor-TEE-yuh)
>Maize-flour pancake or omelette. Beware: ***una tortillere*** = vulgar in Spanish for lesbian.

Toto [Ger]
>***Länder*** or state-controlled football pools in Germany.

totocalcio [It]
>Italian football pools. ***La schedina*** = pools coupon, on which punters have to enter their predictions. ***Fare un tredici*** = a win: all thirteen predictions correct.

toujours [Fr] (too-zhoor)
>Always; for ever.

toujours la politesse [Fr]
>It's always wise to be polite.

tour de force [Fr] (toor duh fohrs)
>A brilliant accomplishment.

Toussaint, La [Fr]
>All Saints' Day, November 1, which is followed on November 2 by ***Le Jour des Morts*** = All Souls' Day when wreaths are placed on graves.

tout à vous [Fr]
>Yours truly.

tout comprende c'est tout pardonner [Fr]
> To understand everything is to forgive everything.

tout court [Fr]
> Briefly; with nothing added; simply.

tout de suite [Fr]
> At once; immediately.

tout ensemble [Fr] (toot ah(n)-SAH(N)-buhl)
> All things considered; the total impression; general effect.

tout ou rien [Fr]
> All or nothing.

traducteur [Fr]
> Translator. *Traduction* = translation.

traduttori traditori [It]
> Translators are traitors; true translation is impossible.

tranche de vie [Fr]
> 'Slice of life'.

trappistenbier [Dut]
> Originally, malt beer brewed by Trappist monks.

trattoria [It]
> Restaurant or *ristorante*.

travailler [Fr]
> To work. *Un travailleur* = labourer; worker.

tredicesima [It]
> Thirteenth. *Tredicesima mensilità*, or *la tredicesima* = the thirteenth or extra month's pay received prior to Christmas.

Treppenwitz [Ger]
> The clever riposte you think of – too late!

tricolore [Fr] (tree-KOL-ohr)
> Three coloured. *Le drapeau tricolore* = the French flag, of *bleu, blanc et rouge*.

tricoteuse [Fr]
> The women who knitted while watching the executions during the French Revolution.

Trinkgeld [Ger]
> In Germany, a tip; gratuity.

tristesse [Fr]
> Sadness; melancholy; gloom; depression.

troika [Rus] (troy-kuh)
> A carriage or sled pulled by three horses; a
> controlling body consisting of three people or
> groups sharing power.

trompe-l'œil [Fr] (tro(m)p luh-yuh)
> A painting that conveys the illusion of reality.

trop de cuisiniers gâtent la sauce [Fr]
> Too many cooks spoil the sauce.

trouvaille [Fr] (troo-vayuh)
> A lucky find; a windfall. ***Trouver l'oiseau*** =
> to find the rare bird; ***trouver la perle*** = to
> find a pearl.

truite [Fr] (trweet)
> Trout. ***Truite saumonée*** = salmon trout.

tsunami [Jap]
> Huge destructive waves caused by submarine
> earthquakes or volcanic eruptions.

Turkish delights

Not to be outdone, Turkey is yet another country
to prove that ***traduttore traditore*** (q.v.). An
Istanbul guide book sets the scene: 'The
circumciser edifications make a fin stroll for all
with a somptuous anfraction. Here old person
can sit in the calme and yong lovers rumble
under some dank and booming tress.' After the
stroll you may retire to your hotel ('ALL
ROOMS WITH FLYING WATER') or engage
a local menu, featuring 'Girled Chaps, Cold Tart
of this House, Savages in Earthwore, Bowels in
Spit, Trousers Stewed and Foul Salad.'

---

tuan [Malay]
> Sir. Polite form of address by Malays.

tulp; **tulpen** [Dut]
> Tulips.

tutte le strade conducono a Roma [It]
> All roads lead to Rome.

tutti-frutti [It] (too-tih froo-tih)
> Fruit ice-cream.

tzatziki [Gk]
> Dip made from cucumber, yoghurt, garlic and oil.

Tziyonut [Heb]
> Zionism. **Tziyoni** = a Zionist.

U

Übermensch [Ger]
> Superior man; a superman.

ubi jus, ibi remedium [Lat]
> Where there is a right there is a remedy.

ubi lapsus? quid feci? [Lat]
> Where did I go wrong? What have I done?

ubi sunt qui ante nos fuerunt? [Lat]
> Where are those who have gone before us?

Übung macht den Meister [Ger]
> Practice makes the master.

ultima Thule [Lat] (UHL-tih-muh TOO-lih)
> The furthest limit; some faraway, unknown region.

ultra vires [Lat] (uhl-truh VEE-rays)
>Beyond the legal powers of a person or
>organization.

Um ein Haar [Ger]
>A close shave.

Umschwung [Ger]
>A sudden change of opinion or direction.

unberufen toi toi toi [Ger]
>An expression equivalent to the English 'touch
>wood' or 'knock on wood'.

uno ictu [Lat]
>At one blow.

uno saltu [Lat]
>With one bound; in a single leap.

un propos sale [Fr]
>A coarse remark.

Unterhosen [Ger]
>Underpants. ***Schlüpfer*** = undershorts. ***Slip*** =
>men's briefs and ladies' knickers; ***die
>Unaussprechlichen*** = the unmentionables.

unter vier Augen [Ger]
>Literally: under four eyes. Between two people
>only; between us; in confidence.

uovo [It]
>Egg. ***Un uovo sodo*** = a hard-boiled egg; ***uova
>strapazzate*** = scrambled eggs.

urbi et orbi [Lat]
>To the city and to the world: the formal
>introduction for papal proclamations and
>blessings.

usus est tyrannus [Lat]
>Fashion or custom is a tyrant.

uyezd [Rus]
>In Russia, a district or county.

V

vade retro, Satana! [Lat]
> Get thee behind me, Satan!

va fan culo [It]
> Extremely vulgar but all too common Italian expression meaning, roughly, 'Up your arse'.

vanitas vanitatum, omnia vanitas [Lat]
> Vanity of vanities, all is vanity.

vase de nuit [Fr]
> Chamber-pot. See ***bourdalou***.

vashe zdarov'ye [Rus]
> Cheers! Used as a toast.

vero? [Lat]
> Really? You think so?

velatorio [Sp]
> Spanish wake – the twenty-four hours preceding a funeral during which the corpse is on view in its coffin.

velouté [Fr]
> A white sauce made with roux and stock.

vendeuse [Fr] (vah(n)-derz)
> Female sales assistant.

veniente occurrite morbo [Lat]
> Meet an approaching sickness; prevention is better than cure.

veni, vidi, vici [Lat]
> I came, I saw, I conquered. Julius Caesar's remark after his victory over Pharnaces.

ventre à terre [Fr] (vah(n)-truh ah-tair)
>Literally: belly to the earth. At full gallop; at full speed.

verbatim et literatim [Lat]
>Word for word, and letter for letter.

verbum sapienti sat est; ***verb. sat***. [Lat]
>A word is enough for the wise. The abbreviation is used as a notice to the reader to take the preceding matter seriously.

veritas nunquam perit [Lat]
>Truth never dies.

veritas omnia vincit [Lat]
>Truth conquers everything. Often written ***vincit omnia veritas***.

Verlag [Ger]
>Publisher; publishing house.

vers de société [Fr]
>Witty topical verse.

vers libre [Fr]
>Unrhymed free verse.

vexata quaestio [Lat]
>A disputed point; an unsettled question.

via [Lat and It]
>By way of; road; street. ***Per via aerea*** = by air mail; ***via mare*** = by sea; ***via terra*** = by land.

Via Crucis [Lat]
>The Stations of the Cross; the fourteen episodes in the Passion of Christ.

via dolorosa [Lat]
>Literally: sorrowful road. A series of distressing experiences. ***Via Dolorosa*** = Christ's route to Calvary and his crucifixion.

via media [Lat]
>A middle course; mid-way between extremes.

vice anglaise
>See *le vice anglais*.

vide [Lat] (vee-day)
>Refer to; see. Used to direct a reader elsewhere in a book, or to another reference.

videlicet; viz [Lat]
> Namely; in other words. The abbreviation is used to introduce an example or explanation.

vie amoureuse [Fr]
> An account of someone's love affairs.

vie manquée [Fr]
> An ill-spent, wasted or misdirected life.

vieux jeu [Fr] (vyu zhu)
> Old-fashioned; out of date.

vieux marcheur [Fr]
> A man, well past it, who still pursues women.

vingt-et-un [Fr] (va(n)-tay-ur(n))
> Twenty-one; blackjack; pontoon.

virgo intacta [Lat]
> A woman who, physically, is still a virgin.

visagisme [Fr]
> Beauty care and make-up. ***Visagiste*** = a beauty expert; cosmetician.

vis medicatrix naturae [Lat]
> Nature's cure; natural recovery from ailments without medicine.

vis-à-vis [Fr] (veez-ah-vee)
> In relation to; regarding; face to face with.

vita brevis, ars longa [Lat]
> Life is short, art is long.

viva voce [Lat] (vi-vuh voh-cheh)
> By word of mouth; orally.

vive la différence! [Fr] (veev lah dee-fah-rah(n)s)
> Long live the difference!: usually applied to the difference between the sexes.

vivir y vivanos [Sp]
> Live and let live.

voilà! [Fr] (vwa-lah)
> There! See! Presto!

vol-au-vent [Fr] (vol-oh-vah(n))
> Small savoury pastries.

volo comparare nonnulla tegumembra [Lat]
> I wish to purchase some condoms.

vox populi [Lat]
>   The voice of the people; public opinion.

voyez! [Fr]
>   Look! See!

W

Wahlverwandtschaft [Ger]
>   An intuitive or natural affinity between two
>   people.

wàiguoren [Ch]
>   Foreigner.

Walpurgisnacht [Ger]
>   Walpurgis Night. The eve of the feast day of St
>   Walpurga (May 1); in German folklore the
>   night of the witch's sabbath.

Weihnachten [Ger]
>   Christmas. ***Heiligabend*** = Christmas Eve.

Weinstube [Ger]
>   German inn, serving wine and beer.

Weltanschauung [Ger]
>   A philosophy of life; a person's philosophical
>   outlook.

Weltschmerz [Ger]
>   Sadness at the ills of the world; sentimentally
>   pessimistic view of the world.

Wénhuà Dàgéming [Ch]
>   The Cultural Revolution.

Wenn die Katze fort ist, tanzen die Mäuse [Ger]
>   When the cat's away, the mice will play.

Wer den Sieg behält, der hat Recht [Ger]
>   The victor is always in the right.

Winespeak

Every week, it seems, a few thousand more people become regular wine drinkers. And why not? The choice of wine today is breathtaking: hundreds of varieties pour in from dozens of countries and thousands of regions and makers. But with the wine comes a culture of wine terminology, most of it expressed in various foreign languages. A full list of all the names and terms you'll find on wine labels would require an encyclopaedia, but here, meanwhile, are some of the more common among them.

Appellation d'Origine Contrôlée [Fr] (ah-pel-AH-syah(n) DOR-rih-zheen korn-TROL-lay)
French legal designation guaranteeing the wine's geographical origin and quality.

blanc de blancs [Fr] (bla(n)-duh-bla(n))
White wine made only from white grapes.

brut [Fr] (broot)
Dry, when applied to sparkling wine.

cave [Fr] (kahv)
Cellar.

cépage [Fr]
The wine grape variety.

cru [Fr]
Growth; applied to a vineyard and the wine it makes.

Denominación de Origen [Sp]
Spanish equivalent of the French AOC (see above).

Denominazione di Origine Controllata [It]	The Italian equivalent of the French AOC (see opposite).
en primeur [Fr]	Buying future wine, still in cask.
flor [Sp]	Literally: flower. A flavour-imparting yeast which is grown in casked wine, usually sherry.
garrafeira [Port]	Portuguese selected, aged wine.
négotiant [Fr]	A merchant who buys wine from growers for blending, ageing, bottling and resale.
mis en bouteille au château [Fr]	Bottled at the château.
Qualitätswein [Ger]	German wine classification for quality wines.
récoltant [Fr]	Wine grower.
Spätlese [Ger] (shpayt-layzuh)	Wine from sweet late-harvested grapes.
Tafelwein [Ger]	Table wine.
vinho verde [Port]	Green or young wine. ***Vinho maduro*** = wine that has aged.
Vins Délimités de Qualité Superiéure; ***VDQS*** [Fr]	Controlled French wine category not quite up to the AOC standard.

Wer ein Kalb stiehlt, stiehlt eine Kuh [Ger]
>He who steals a calf, steals a cow.

Wider den Strom schwimmen ist schwer [Ger]
>It's harder to swim agains the current; don't
>kick against the pricks.

wunderbar [Ger] (voon-duh-bar)
>Wonderful.

Wunderkind [Ger] (voon-duh-kint)
>A child prodigy.

Wurst [Ger]
>Sausage. ***Blutwurst*** = black pudding;
>***Bockwurst*** = pink sausage;
>***Schinkenwurst*** = ham sausage; ***Bratwurst*** =
>fried ***Bockwurst***.

X

Xianggang [Ch]
>Hong Kong.

Xizang [Ch]
>Tibet.

Y

yad rochetset yad [Heb]
> You help me, I help you.

Yahadut [Heb]
> Judaism.

yakitori [Jap]
> Skewered chicken cooked on a grill.

yarmulka; yarmulke [Yid]
> Skull-cap worn by Orthodox Jewish males.

yashmak [Arab]
> Face-concealing veil worn by Muslim women.

yeftah allah [Arab]
> The words that accompany an offer – usually well under the vendor's price – that a buyer is willing to pay, without giving offence.

yehudi [Heb]
> Jewish.

yenta [Yid]
> A crude, loud, female gossip.

yerushalayim [Heb]
> Jerusalem.

Yinggélán [Ch]
> England. **Yingguó** = Britain.

Yom Kippur [Heb]
> Annual Jewish Day of Atonement religious holiday.

yoni [Sanskrit]
> In Hinduism, the venerated female genitalia.

Yiddish

Yiddish, a blend of mostly German and some Hebrew, migrated during the last century to America where, even today, it continues to colour American-English. *Fancy-schmancy* is fifth generation *Yidglish* but true Yiddishisms still surface. If you're called a *schmendrik*, start worrying; it means you think you're fantastic and cool but actually you've got a big hole in your pants and you haven't noticed. Even so, it is better than being a *bupkiss* – a nothing.

Apart from its colour, Yiddish has a questioning quality: the propensity to answer a question with a question. Why do Yiddish speakers do this? Why shouldn't they? The answer lies in Genesis 4:9 – '. . . the Lord said unto Cain, where is Abel thy brother?' And what does Cain say? 'Am I my brother's keeper?'. A true Yiddisher.

Z

zabaglione [It] (zab-ah-lih-OH-nih)
>   Whipped dessert of egg yolks, sugar and Marsala wine.

zapateado [Sp]
>   The fast footwork and stamping feet of Spanish dancing.

Zeitgeist [Ger] (tzeyt-guyst)
> The attitude of a period; the spirit of the time.

Zeitung [Ger]
> Newspaper; journal.

zhela-yoo oodachee! [Rus]
> Good luck!

Zhongguo [Ch]
> China. ***Zhongguo rénmín*** = the Chinese people.

Zijincheng [Ch]
> The Forbidden City.

zinc [Fr]
> Colloquial for the 'counter' in a bar or café. ***Manger sur le zinc*** = eating/ drinking at the counter.

Zivilcourage [Ger]
> To have the courage of one's convictions and to express them without fear.

zizi [Fr]
> Slang for either male or female genitalia.

zuppa [It]
> Soup. ***Zuppa di verdura*** = vegetable soup; ***zuppa di pesce*** = fish soup.

Zwieback [Ger] (zwee-bahk)
> Baked bread rusk.

Thirteen-Phrase Survival Guide in Thirteen Languages

You suddenly, unexpectedly, find yourself in a strange country. You don't understand what the natives are saying and they can't understand you. You revert to primitive sign language, trying to explain who you are, that (you point to empty pockets) you have no money, that you need help. But sign language isn't enough. You desperately need just a few words and phrases to ease the way to understanding.

The following rough survival guide – just thirteen expressions – provides the most elementary key to getting out of such a hypothetical situation in thirteen countries.

But don't suddenly, unexpectedly, land yourself in China. The complexities of translating Pinyin and its four tones are, regrettably, beyond the ultra-simplified format of our little Survival Guide.

ENGLISH	FRENCH	GERMAN
Yes	*oui*	*ja*
No	*non*	*nein*
Please	*s'il vous plaît*	*bitte*
Thank you	*merci*	*danke*
No, thanks	*non merci*	*nein danke*
Sorry	*pardon*	*verzeihung*
Can you help me?	*Est-ce que vous pouvez m'aider?*	*Können Sie mir bitte helfen?*
I don't understand	*Je ne comprends pas*	*Ich verstehe nicht*
I don't speak ...	*Je ne parle pas français*	*Ich spreche wenig Deutsch*
Do you speak English?	*Est-ce que vous parlez anglais?*	*Sprechen Sie Englisch?*
Where is the toilet?	*Où sont les toilettes?*	*Wo ist die Toilette?*
Goodbye	*au revoir*	*auf Wiedersehen*
Get lost!	*va t'en!*	*gehen Sie weg!*

SPANISH	ITALIAN	RUSSIAN
si	*si*	*da*
no	*no*	*nyet*
por favor	*per favore*	*pazhalsta*
gracias	*grazie*	*spasiba*
no, gracias	*no grazie*	*nyet spasiba*
lo siento	*mi dispiace*	*prasteet-ye*
Me puede ayudar?	*può aiutarmi?*	*vi mozhet-ye mn-ye pamoch?*
No comprendo	*non capisco*	*ya nye paneema-yoo*
No hablo Español	*non parlo Italiano*	*ya nye gavaryoo pa-ruskee*
Habla usted Inglés?	*Parla Inglese?*	*Vi gavaret-ye pa-Angleeskee?*
Donde están los servicios?	*C'è un gabinetto?*	*Gd-ye too-alyet?*
adios	*arrivederci*	*da sveedanee-ya*
Vayase!	*Vattene!*	*Ookhadeet-ye!*

ENGLISH	PORTUGUESE	SWEDISH
Yes	*sim*	*ja*
No	*não*	*nej*
Please	*por favor*	*yar s god*
Thank you	*obrigado*	*tack*
No, thanks	*não obrigado*	*nej tack*
Sorry	*desculp*	*förlat*
Can you help me?	*pode-me ajudar?*	*kan du hjälpa mig?*
I don't understand	*não compreendo*	*Jag förstår inte*
I can't speak ...	*eu não falo Portugues*	*Jag talar inte Svenska*
Do you speak English?	*Fala Inglês?*	*Talar du Engelska?*
Where is the toilet?	*Ondee é a casa de banho?*	*Var är toalett?*
Goodbye	*adeus*	*adjö*
Get lost!	*Vã'se embora!*	*förs vinn!*

GREEK	HUNGARIAN	DUTCH
ne	igen	ja
ochi	nem	neen/nee
parakalo	kérem	alstublieft
efkharisto	köszönöm	dank u
ochi efkharisto	köszönöm nem	nee, dank u
signomi	elnézést	net spijt mij
boris na me voithisis?	kérhetem a segítségét?	kunt u mij helpen?
Then katalaveno	Nem ertem	Ik begrijp het niet
Then milao Elinika	Nem beszélek Magyarul	Ik spreek geen Nederlands
Milate Aglika?	Beszél angolul?	Spreekt u Engels?
Poo ini i toualeta?	Hol van a WC/árnyékszék?	Waar zijn de toiletten?
andio	viszontlátásra	tot ziens
fiye!	hagyjou békén!	ga weg!

ENGLISH	HEBREW	JAPANESE
Yes	*ken*	*hai*
No	*lo*	*iya*
Please	*bewakaschar*	*doozo*
Thank you	*todah*	*domo arigato*
No, thanks	*lo todah*	*kekko des arigato*
Sorry	*slik-ha*	*sumi-masen*
Can you help me?	*efshah la'azor li?*	*choto sumi-masen?*
I don't understand	*ani lo mevin*	*Wakarimasen*
I can't speak ...	*ani lo medaber*	*Nihongo wa hanasemasen*
Do you speak English?	*Ata medaber Anglit?*	*Eigo a hanashimass ka?*
Where is the toilet?	*Ayfo hasheruh?*	*toiret wa doko dess ka?*
Goodbye	*shalom*	*sayonara*
Get lost!	*lekh mi-po!*	*atchi e it-to!*

ARABIC

naam

laa

min fadlek

shoukran

laa shoukran

aasef

min fadlek, momken tosa-aadnih?

Ma-afham

Ma aqdar atakalam Arabee

Hal tatakalam Engleezi?

wa-yu at-towaalet?

maa as-salaamah

emshee!

A Full List of Titles Available from Mandarin in this series

While every effort is made to keep prices low, it is sometimes necessary to increase prices at short notice. Mandarin Paperbacks reserves the right to show new retail prices on covers which may differ from those previously advertised in the text or elsewhere.

The prices shown below were correct at the time of going to press.

All these books are available at your bookshop or newsagent, or can be ordered direct from the address below. Just tick the titles you want and fill in the form below.

Cash Sales Department, PO Box 5, Rushden, Northants NN10 6YX.

Please send cheque, payable to 'Reed Book Services Ltd.', or postal order for purchase price quoted and allow the following for postage and packing:

£1.00 for the first book, 50p for the second; **FREE POSTAGE AND PACKING FOR THREE BOOKS OR MORE PER ORDER.**

NAME (Block letters) ....

ADDRESS ....

....

☐ I enclose my remittance for ....

☐ I wish to pay by Access/Visa Card Number

Expiry Date